PLANTOPEDIA

LAUREN CAMILLERI & SOPHIA KAPLAN OF *LEAF SUPPLY*

PLANTOPEDIA

The Definitive Guide to Houseplants

Smith
Street
Books

FOR FRANKIE + RAFI
THE NEXT GENERATION OF PLANT LOVERS

contents

Connecting with plants

The process of nurturing life (plant or person) is driven by an innately human desire. The benefits of this connection to plants, in our increasingly urban lives, are not to be overlooked.

For many of us living in inner-city apartments with limited access to greenery, and even for those living in more suburban or rural areas, caring for and tending to plants in our homes is something we should eagerly embrace.

Growing and looking after an indoor garden is rewarding; a therapeutic endeavour that can help foster a better relationship with the natural world. At a time when negative human impact on the environment has never been more apparent, appreciating the value of nature and how it sustains us is of the utmost importance. Perhaps this goes some way to explaining the increasing popularity of indoor gardening in recent times. Now, more than ever, we need to reassess the way we live and learn how we can tread more lightly on our planet.

Plantopedia is an accessible and modern indoor-plant encyclopedia that we hope will help cultivate this human connection to plants. We profile a comprehensive range of foliage plants, succulents and cacti, from readily available varieties to rarer unicorns that will appeal to everyone from novice gardeners to horticultural experts. We look at each genus before deep-diving into individual species, to inspire you to either start or expand your own plant collection. All plants are,

of course, naturally outdoor organisms, and when we refer to houseplants we are speaking of those that enjoy the conditions provided by being inside our living and working spaces. Thankfully for us, there are many foliage and succulent varieties that live happily indoors, from aroids, ferns and begonias to *Rhipsalis* and *Euphorbia*. When caring for plants, it's best to try to mimic their natural environment, so it is important to understand where they originate, as well as how they grow in the wild. The key to success is to choose plant varieties that are best suited to the specific conditions in your space. Once you know what you're dealing with, you are in a good position to select species that will thrive.

All plants are, of course, naturally outdoor organisms, and when we refer to houseplants we are speaking of those that enjoy the conditions provided by being inside our living and working spaces.

For ease of use we have created a detailed key that covers all the essentials: care level, light, water, soil, humidity, propagation, growth habit, positioning and toxicity. We troubleshoot any plant issues you might come across and discuss common pests and diseases that can invade your collection. Armed with this knowledge, you will be able to manage and understand your plants' life cycles and their beautiful imperfections. Up the back, a plant care index makes navigating the plant profiles a breeze and a stunning visual index groups plants based on their care requirements so you can easily pick and choose the right plants for you and the space you live in. We've also included a helpful glossary to refer to if there are any terms you're unsure of as you make your way through the book.

With access to the collections of some incredibly passionate plant people, we have been able to photograph most of the plants profiled in this book. These striking portraits illustrate the myriad shapes, textures, colours and beauty of the indoor plant world. While this book is by no means exhaustive, it's a comprehensive guide for indoor gardeners of all levels. We hope it will educate and inspire you to nurture your own indoor oasis and perhaps grow your collection. We encourage you to share your plants with our Leaf Supply community by tagging @leaf_supply and using the hashtag #plantopedia so we can share in your plant pursuits. Now go forth and garden!

History of houseplants

Cultivating plants for pleasure is not new. Around 600 BCE, the fabled Hanging Gardens of Babylon were one of the earliest written records of a garden created purely for its aesthetic beauty rather than the necessity of growing food. The story goes that King Nebuchadnezzar II commissioned the gardens for his wife, Queen Amytis, who missed the lush greenery of her home in Persia. What a guy! The resulting gardens resembled the verdant mountains of her birthplace, filled with olive, quince, pistachio, pear, date and fig trees. Mysteriously, even though the Hanging Gardens are one of the Seven Wonders of the Ancient World, their exact location has never been discovered, and with conflicting accounts about their origin and no archaeological proof of their existence, these gardens may always remain a beautiful myth.

There are, however, well-documented accounts from Ancient Egypt, Greece and Rome of wealthy citizens tending to plants in their sprawling estates, either indoors or in their courtyards, often with a focus on edible and flowering species. Over in Asia, the art of Bonsai, where small trees are cultivated to mimic the shape and scale of full-size trees, began in China between the 2nd and 5th centuries CE.

In Europe, the popularity of houseplants is thought to have declined after the fall of the Western Roman Empire in the 5th century CE until the start of the Renaissance in the late 14th century when they came back into vogue in a big way. As European countries ravaged and colonised the Americas, Africa, Asia and Oceania, they also brought back with them botanical specimens for the purposes of growing food, scientific study, commercial production and display. The rich began to showcase their wealth by growing plants in orangeries (early greenhouses), which allowed citrus as well as other tropical plants to be grown in colder climates.

But while the wealthy have long enjoyed the pleasure of houseplants, it wasn't until the 19th century that the pursuit spread to the middle classes. As increasing numbers of tropical and subtropical plants were imported from across the globe, the fashion for houseplants peaked. *Aspidistra*, for example, described by British botanist John Bellenden Ker Gawler in 1822, was introduced to the UK where it earned the common name 'cast-iron plant' because it was capable of surviving in even the darkest of homes. As glass became more readily available, conservatories began popping up in English gardens, and by the 20th century, advances in lighting and heating allowed for an even greater variety of plants to be grown indoors.

As with all things, the popularity of indoor plants has waxed and waned. The start of the 20th century saw a shift in attitudes as modernity entered the home and the plant-filled interiors of Victorian England seemed decidedly old-fashioned. The architectural forms of cacti and succulents fitted more appropriately with the style of the day and their appeal grew. By the end of World War II, there was again a proliferation in the popularity of indoor plants as they livened up the often drab and sterile workplaces of the time. These hardy plants, tolerant of low-light conditions, soon migrated to homes where people were increasingly living in apartments. This, along with the rise in popularity of Scandinavian design, including the Swedish passion for indoor plants, such as the Swiss cheese plant and lush Boston fern, saw yet another revival in the 1970s.

Fast forward to the 2020s and houseplants are, once again, back in the limelight where they rightly belong. Recent studies have shown that houseplants increase concentration, productivity and general well-being, meaning that hopefully they are here to stay, as we learn to appreciate the huge benefits of living with greenery.

A NOTE ON THE HISTORY OF BOTANY

In addition to acknowledging the often white, Western role in the world of botany and horticulture, we feel a greater discussion is needed about the ways in which the science was established, often at the detriment of First Nations people. In the pursuit of cultivating economic crops for empire building, local inhabitants were often exploited for labour, and their history and knowledge of local botany was ignored or erased. Despite the language commonly used by many of us, it stands to reason that European botanists were not the first to 'discover' certain plants, rather they were the first to record them using Western methodologies. This is indeed a complex issue, and there is a lot of learning to be done within the industry to address the history of many national botanical collections around the world. We all need to educate ourselves about the true narrative and listen more deeply to First Nations people in an effort to make the world, and our plant-loving community, a more equal place.

Plant classification

In the 18th century, Swedish botanist Carl Linneaus invented binomial nomenclature, the system for identifying organisms using two Latin or scientific names: one to signify genus; the other to denote individual species within that genus.

Prior to the creation of the binomial system, plants were named according to how individuals saw and described them. In many cases, plant names would be five to ten words long and based purely on observation. Linneaus's international naming convention allowed plant collectors the world over to identify plants without confusion or contention.

Conversely, common plant names, in their truest form, arise, unsurprisingly, from common use, often by individuals who are not aware of scientific naming conventions. There is no international protocol governing the way common plant names should be written or used and, therefore, they differ greatly from country to country. For many of us, it is the locally assigned common names that we are most likely to recognise and use to refer to the plants we know. While you have probably never heard of the *Nephrolepis exaltata*, you may actually have one in your house better known to you by its common name, Boston fern. Botanical names can seem complicated and overly scientific at first, but they're actually relatively simple and incredibly useful once you get a hang of the rules and terminology.

As mentioned, the first scientific name refers to a plant's genus, which is the collective name for a group of plants that share the same (or occasionally similar) floral characteristics. The 'specific epithet' follows in lower-case and distinguishes the species within the genus. Convention dictates that Latin names are always italicised (or underlined if handwritten) with the genus capitalised. For example, the Latin name for the Swiss cheese plant is *Monstera deliciosa*. '*Monstera*' refers to the genus and '*deliciosa*' references the delicious-tasting fruit the plant produces. In addition, it is acceptable to refer to a collection of *Monstera* species as *Monstera* sp. (which is short for the plural form of species). Learning the meaning of specific epithets helps to reveal not only where a plant comes from and what conditions it likes, but also its growth habits and the common characteristics the plant is likely to exhibit.

There are a number of hierarchical levels of classification above and below each genus and species, such as the grouping of several genera into a family. While the plants within a family may look very different, they share common ancestors and characteristics that bind them. Below the classification of species there is the subspecies, variety, cultivar or hybrid.

A subspecies is a distinct variant of a species, usually based on geographical location. Isolation from the true species means that the subspecies will often adopt different physical characteristics. This is noted as subsp. or ssp. after the species epithet and it is always lower-case and not italicised.

Plant varieties arise in a number of ways, but they are always naturally occurring. A variety (noted by 'var.' and italicised) displays some kind of variation from the true species – for example, exhibiting giant flowers (var. *grandiflora*) or tiny fruits (var. *microcarpus*) – but otherwise the plants are exactly the same. Varietals occur either from a random genetic mutation on a plant, or from growing seeds produced by a fertilised plant.

A cultivar, on the other hand, refers to a new plant that has been produced by humans through cultivation, rather than occurring naturally in the wild. Cultivar names are listed in lower-case (unless including a person or place name), they are never italicised and always presented in single quotation marks. Often, they are named after the person who bred or discovered the plant, or after a significant feature of the plant. Due to a decades-old ruling by the ICBN (International Code of Binomial Nomenclature for algae, fungi and plants), cultivar names can no longer be Latinised to avoid confusion with varieties and subspecies.

Finally, the cross fertilisation of two plants results in a hybrid, also known as a cross or a crossbreed. Most hybrid plants are intentional crosses, involving a great deal of work and many attempts to produce the desired results. Hybridisation, however, can also occur in nature when two nearby plants of different species cross-pollinate via insects or the wind. The resulting seeds fall on the soil and grow into a hybrid. While a hybrid can be named, there is no requirement that a hybrid name should be created for plants that are believed to be of hybrid origin. They may instead be described using a formula that lists the parents, separated by the multiplication sign.

Identification of organisms has long been an inexact science. As a result, plants have commonly switched genera, sometimes being reclassified a number of times. The recent advent of genetic testing has seen these shifts increase and it stands to reason that much more will occur as this technique for identification is more widely employed. We have endeavoured to list the most current classifications, and when plants have changed genus, we make mention of their taxonomic origins, listing the synonym (the now outdated name for the species, noted as syn.) as one of the additional common names.

Cultivation

Most of us have an interest and appreciation for where our food comes from, and we believe the same should go for plants.

There's a lot of thought, love and hard work that goes into researching, growing and selecting the plants that make it into nurseries and plant shops like our own, and then onwards into your home or office. Indoor plants are cultivated by a network of growers around the world who research, spot trends, cultivate and nurture baby plants into the healthy specimens you find at your local plant store. Visiting nurseries to source plants is one of the most rewarding parts of our job – you haven't really breathed fresh air until you enter a greenhouse full of lush, green foliage. Seeing the swathes of greenery, sneaking peeks at new varieties growing in hidden greenhouses and chatting to growers is always exciting and inspiring.

During our research for this book, we spoke to three of our favourite Sydney-based nurserymen – Keith Wallace (who's been a grower for 42 years!) and Gordon Giles of Keith Wallace Nursery, and Jeremy Critchley of The Green Gallery – about everything that's involved.

"Deciding what plants to grow is one of the toughest parts of the business – and one of the most enjoyable," says Jeremy, who regularly travels overseas to visit nurseries and trade shows to see what's on trend elsewhere in the world. "Every year plant trends and demand for certain lines change. It goes up and down very quickly. What was the biggest thing last year, is now just a run-of-the-mill indoor plant that you can find in chain stores."

Most nurseries in Australia grow from a combination of cuttings, seeds and tissue culture. Some ferns are also grown via spore propagation. Cuttings are a type of propagation that generally come from more local sources (having originally been "imported by enthusiasts", says Keith), whereas tissue culture is often sourced overseas and involves plant tissues being grown in a lab. This helps to create a clean and virus-free specimen, which in turn makes them more viable to grow in large numbers and easier to comply with quarantine laws.

Jeremy explains the process of sourcing tissue culture: "I travel overseas to visit tissue culture labs to see what they have coming through the pipeline, and to give recommendations as to what to put in. The majority of these labs are in Southeast Asia and China, but we also work with labs in South America, USA and Europe.

I also travel to plant markets and nurseries to see if there are any cool plants that I haven't seen in production before, and then I'll ask the local lab to try and extract tissue culture from them to see if we can make a commercial variety. I have been lucky enough to visit some amazing botanical gardens in Indonesia where I've spoken with curators and lab managers to see if there are any 'straight-from-the-jungle' species that are worth growing."

"I think it will stop being a trend and people will realise that indoor plants are a necessity in their lives – there are so many positives to having them in your space."

Most nurseries grow a selection of classic, ever-popular plants while experimenting with new and interesting varieties. For the new varieties, it's always a bit of a gamble as to what will be popular and what will end up on the compost pile. As Jeremy explains, "It's quite a long process from finding a funky plant in a tree in Indonesia, to having it available for purchase in a retail outlet in Australia. It's probably a minimum of two years, often three. It takes the lab a good four to six months to clean the plants and get them ready for culture, another six months to successfully grow the culture and then at least another six months to build up some decent numbers. Once in Australia, it takes seven to 14 months to grow the plants. It's a super-long time and the wait feels like forever. Sometimes, even after all that work and time, a plant is still not a winner. You just never know! That's why some of the new releases are very expensive at the beginning – the amount of work, resources, time and money that goes into them is significant."

Keith, on the other hand, grows 90 per cent of his plants from division or stem cuttings. He says, "On average the journey takes 12–15 months from cutting to mature plant. The young plants remain in trays in greenhouses equipped with misting systems and coolers (plus heating in winter) for an average of four to six months (depending on the time of year), before we pot up. Normally we grow them for another six months before they are mature enough to be sold to retail outlets."

Gordon, the master of *Cymbidium* (boat orchids), must show even greater patience. He has devoted a lifetime (66 years to be precise) to hybridising these beautiful plants, which take an average of seven years from seed to flower.

We love watching the way plants are nurtured by all the nurserymen and women, as they try to emulate as closely as possible their native environment. Plants are given custom potting mix, top-quality fertilisers and regular watering to ensure they have the best start in life. Keith believes the key factors are "good light, adequate water and air circulation, along with making sure the growing areas are clean". Hygiene is so important to ensure that young plants aren't overcome by pests and diseases, although, interestingly, the environment at The Green Gallery isn't sterile; instead,

Jeremy's team inoculate their plants with a variety of beneficial bacteria and fungi. "The plants have a strong symbiotic relationship with these microorganisms. That means less disease, more nutrient uptake and, as in nature, a complete soil biology to help the plants grow and be happy. We use as few chemical sprays as possible (significantly less than what is used in larger traditional nurseries), and we release a variety of beneficial insects to combat any pests that might make their way into our production areas," explains Jeremy. We love this approach to gardening.

Jeremy is encouraged by all the young people getting into plants and horticulture. "I think soon it will stop being a trend and people will realise that indoor plants are a necessity in their lives – there are so many positives to having them in your space." He has a great mentality when it comes to indoor gardening: "People need to understand that plants are a biological entity and that sadly not every plant they buy and grow will be successful. For various reasons, some plants will just not work for people in certain places. But don't give up – there's a plant for every situation and every person."

We couldn't agree more and we will always advocate buying plants from reputable growers who treat their plants and their staff with kindness.

Cheilanthes japonica
Japanese Bamboo Fern

Doryopteris ludens

How to use this book

Plantopedia profiles more than 130 of our favourite houseplants, from tropical leafy varieties to desert-dwelling succulents and cacti, and all those that fall somewhere in between. We cover the stalwarts of the indoor-plant scene, as well as many rare and remarkable varieties. Every plant has a unique personality and, therefore, varying care requirements, and we're here to help you establish which plants are the best fit for you and your space. Are you a houseplant virgin or do you have a track record of plant homicide? Then we recommend you start with something super-easy to care for, such as devil's ivy. Successfully kept a fiddle-leaf fig alive for more than a year? Then you're ready to move on to something a little more needy, so hello calatheas! Got yourself a greenhouse? Then the world is your oyster; go nuts and try the carnivorous *Nepenthes*.

To make this book as practical as possible, we have created a key that provides vital information about each plant. This is especially useful for those just getting started with indoor gardening. Basic care requirements regarding light, soil and water are included, as is information about growth habits, propagation, plant positioning and toxicity to our furry friends. We have also grouped plants according to their care level (check out our handy visual index at the back of the book).

Here's how it works ...

CARE LEVEL

From the lowest of low-maintenance plants to the divas of the foliage world, there is a plant for every skill level. By all means experiment with any plant that tickles your fancy but know that, like humans, some plants are more work than others.

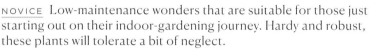

NOVICE Low-maintenance wonders that are suitable for those just starting out on their indoor-gardening journey. Hardy and robust, these plants will tolerate a bit of neglect.

GREEN THUMB These plants require a little more attention and effort, but there's no reason why they shouldn't thrive in the right conditions and with the appropriate care.

EXPERT The drama queens of the plant world. Save these plants for when you've got a bit of plant parenthood experience under your belt.

LIGHT

When it comes to plants, light is life! When we bring greenery inside we need to try and mimic as closely as possible their natural habitat, providing them with the essential light that powers their growth through the process of photosynthesis. Does the plant naturally grow at the base of a forest in dappled sunlight? If so, lots of bright, indirect light and some gentle direct morning or late afternoon rays will be best. If it hails from the desert, it will likely need a solid amount of direct sun to keep it happy. Thankfully, there are also some plants that tolerate low-light environments as well.

Understanding the light conditions of your space is key. To start, identify all available light sources and then take note of how the light moves through each space over the course of the day. The orientation of your space as well as any surrounding buildings or window coverings will also help you determine the level of light that reaches your indoor plants. A spot closest to windows and skylights will be the brightest, especially if the plant can see the sky from its position. Light meter apps, which you can download onto your smartphone, are a great tool to discover what you're working with.

While there are a number of plants that will tolerate lower-light conditions, it is important to note that most will need a bright spot to really thrive. For plants residing mostly in the darker corners of your home, we recommend giving them a monthly holiday somewhere bright, if possible. Also keep in mind that light conditions change with the seasons, so be sure to rotate your plants as required to sunnier spots during the cooler, darker months, and vice versa in spring and summer.

LOW-MODERATE Tolerant of lower-light conditions, but will thrive in bright, indirect light.

BRIGHT, INDIRECT Enjoys a position that receives plenty of diffuse bright light, with access to direct morning sun if available. Avoid any harsh afternoon sun that will burn foliage.

FULL SUN These sun worshippers (think desert cacti, such as the golden-barrel cactus) require lots of direct rays to thrive indoors.

WATER

In terms of a plant's needs, coming in at a close second is water. Unlike in the wild where plants rely on mother nature to keep them hydrated, indoor plants rely solely on us. There are a number of variables that can affect the amount of water a plant needs, including its variety, the amount of light it gets (generally speaking the greater the light, the higher the water needs), ambient temperature, airflow and circulation, potting mix and the size and type of container in which it's planted.

The best way to determine if your plant needs a drink is to get your finger in the soil once or twice a week and have a feel. While it might help forgetful plant parents to choose a specific day of the week to water, you run the risk of over- or under-watering your plant babies. For those who are a little less confident, a water metre can be helpful. They're cheap, easy to use and will give you a clear reading of whether your plant is ready to be watered again. This method allows you to respond directly to your plants' needs and establish a consistent watering regime.

For container plants with drainage holes, water deeply and directly into the soil, until you see water flowing from the base. You want to ensure that all the roots have been wetted. This can be done over the sink, in the shower or outside. For those pots with saucers, be sure to empty any overflow sitting more than 30 minutes after watering, to keep water away from roots and reduce the risk of root rot developing.

While most indoor plants will happily tolerate tap water (room temperature is best), it can lead to a build-up of certain minerals in the soil. When possible, try and get your plants out in the rain or collect some rainwater in a bucket or watering can to bring inside. For fussier plants (*Nepenthes* and *Tillandsia* are particularly picky), it's important to use distilled water.

LOW Plants with thick succulent leaves and stems (that is most succulents and cacti) have the capacity to store water in their bodies and thus require less water than their leafy friends. Water when the majority of the soil has dried out. This may be about every two weeks in spring and summer and once a month in the cooler seasons.
MODERATE Many foliage plants fall into this category. Water when the top 5 cm (2 in) of soil has dried out. This is approximately once a week in spring and summer and less frequently in autumn and winter.
HIGH These plants prefer evenly moist soil – we're looking at you, maidenhair fern! Water when just the soil surface has dried out.

SOIL

Good-quality, well-suited potting mix is a crucial foundation that will nurture strong, healthy growth in your indoor jungle. Facilitating a plant's absorption of water and nutrients, as well as providing adequate drainage, the right potting mix gives your plants the best chance to thrive.

It is perfectly acceptable to buy potting mix from your local hardware store or nursery, but be sure to choose the highest-quality organic indoor potting mix. Store-bought potting mix generally has enough nutrients to support happy growth for six to 12 months. After this, you'll need to start adding your own fertiliser. We recommend using a diluted organic liquid fertiliser for your indoor pals.

WELL-DRAINING Standard premium potting mix that allows water to drain easily. The addition of perlite opens up the soil for better airflow and reduces moisture retention.

MOISTURE-RETAINING A potting mix that retains moisture with the inclusion of coir or coco peat. Avoid mixes that contain peat moss, the harvesting of which is environmentally harmful.

COARSE + SANDY A potting mix with a high content of sand and grit, which allows water to quickly drain away from the roots – perfect for desert dwellers.

HUMIDITY

Many of the plants that live happily in our homes hail from the rainforest where things are decidedly humid. Greenhouses, in which most indoor plants will spend time before they make their way to retail stores and then to us, provide the ideal growing environment for indoor plants, where diffuse light from above abounds and humidity is high. Our homes on the other hand are generally fairly dry environments and this change can be quite a shock to the system for new plants. If humidity is really low (often due to air conditioning or heating), a plant's roots will struggle to absorb an adequate amount of water to keep up with the moisture lost through the leaves.

As a general rule, the thinner the leaf, the greater its need for humidity. Thick, leathery or waxy leaves, or those covered with hair, are usually relatively immune to dry air. While succulents and cacti can deal with much drier conditions, both above and below the surface, tropical plants enjoy a relative humidity of around 50 per cent.

There are a few things you can do to manage low humidity. One solution is to regularly spritz your plants' leaves with a water mister. This is best done in the morning and with tepid water so the foliage has a chance to dry out during the day (good ventilation will assist here, too.) Sitting your humidity-loving plants on a saucer filled with pebbles and water is another useful trick. This creates a moister environment around the plant while ensuring that it isn't sitting in a pool of water potentially causing root rot. Grouping plants together can also increase the moisture levels around foliage by creating a microclimate that helps boost humidity. If you're really serious about providing your indoor plants with the steamy jungle conditions they so desire, then a humidifier is the way to go.

NONE Encompassing cacti and most succulents, these plants prefer dry conditions and will not tolerate misting, which can lead to fungal issues and other problems.

LOW Mist plants weekly in summer, if you like, but ultimately they will be fine without.

MEDIUM Many common indoor plants benefit from a spritz once a day or so. Try to group plants with similar humidity requirements together and consider sitting them on a pebble tray filled with water.

HIGH We refer to these as 'humidifier plants'. High-maintenance varieties, such as many anthuriums and those sensitive tuberous begonias, which require high levels of ambient humidity but won't tolerate water on their leaves. Such levels can't be achieved in our homes without the help of a humidifier.

PROPAGATING

Plants are intrinsically built to grow and multiply. Whether you're looking to expand your own collection or share the love with friends, propagating is an inexpensive and easy way to get new plants from your existing collection.

When setting out to propagate plants it's important to note that success is definitely not guaranteed, so don't be discouraged if some cuttings don't make it. Here are some things to consider to encourage successful propagation.

- Choose the healthiest plant. The exception to the rule here is if you have a plant that you are trying to salvage by propagating. In which case you really have nothing to lose.
- Propagation is best done in the warmer months when plants are in their active growing period.
- Water your chosen plant a couple of days before propagating, so it's nice and hydrated.
- Rainwater or distilled water is preferred when propagating.
- Take more cuttings than you need as not all will take.
- Handle cuttings gently when separating them from the original plant.
- Don't over-water cuttings or place them in too large a pot while the roots are settling in, as this can drown your plant.
- Keep baby plants in a warm, brightly lit spot without any direct sunlight.

To get started, all you need is a plant that's ready for propagating; clean, sharp secateurs; clean pots filled with potting or seedling mix; or glass vessels (depending on which method you're using). For those new to propagating, keep it simple and start with devil's ivy cuttings in a glass. Below and over the page, we explore four techniques suitable for different varieties of indoor plants. Plants can be propagated using one or sometimes more of the methods below, so check the plant profile for specific info.

STEM CUTTINGS Probably the most common propagation technique that works well for lots of plants, including aroids, begonias and hoyas. Using a clean pair of secateurs, cut your stem at a 45 degree angle, ensuring it's about 10 cm (4 in) long and includes a few leaves and one or two nodes (ridges on the stem, often alongside a leaf or side shoot). Most tropical plants can be placed directly into a fresh pot filled with potting mix, seedling mix or coco coir; or into a water-filled glass vessel. Unlike tropical plants, most cacti and succulent cuttings should be left to callus (dry out) for a few days before planting into a coarse, sandy potting mix. Allowing the cut end to 'seal' also means it's less likely to become infected. You can further increase your chances of success by dipping the callused end into a store-bought rooting hormone, or use a natural substitute like honey or even saliva! Just spit on a plate rather than insert the cutting into your mouth. New roots can take up to six weeks to appear, so be patient!

PLANTLETS + OFFSETS Plantlets are miniature versions of the adult plant that appear at the ends of branches and runners. Spider plants are a perfect example, producing lots of baby spiders on aerial stems from the mother plant. Similarly, offsets are side shoots or 'pups' that are genetically identical daughter plants, produced by plants such as the Chinese money plant (*Pilea peperomiodes*) or snake plant (*Dracaena trifasciata*). These baby plants usually appear around the base of the mother plant and are very delicate with only a small number of roots. Once plantlets and offsets are a decent size, simply remove them with a clean, sharp knife or secateurs and place in a fresh pot with good-quality potting mix and adequate drainage. Both can also be rooted successfully in water.

LEAF CUTTINGS This technique works well for plants such as succulents and begonias. Gently twist off a leaf at the stem, making sure to remove the whole leaf. Let the leaf dry out for one to three days to lessen its chance of rotting, then dip it in your choice of rooting hormone and insert two-thirds of the stem end into the soil. Point the leaves away from the middle of the pot so the new roots are centred, and gently press the potting mix down.

DIVISION Once some plants are big enough, you can easily divide them to create two or more plants. It's best to do this in early spring so your new plants will have a burst of growth once they've been repotted. To start, remove the original plant from its pot, then grab the plant with both hands and gently try to pull it apart. If this fails, remove the soil from the roots and try again, or use a knife to carefully separate the roots. Then all you have to do is pop each new division into a fresh pot and top it up with new potting mix. Make sure you treat these new plants gently for a couple of weeks, watering them regularly and keeping out of direct light. Calatheas and peace lilies are good examples of plants that can be propagated using this method.

GROWTH HABIT

Understanding the form your plant will take as it grows can help inform not only where you position it, but also the most suitable vessel, as well as any maintenance that might be required including staking or regular repotting.

UPRIGHT Straight, strong stems that reach towards the ceiling.
CLIMBING Plants that naturally climb trees or other surfaces in the wild.
TRAILING Plants with stems that dangle over the edge of pots and elegantly trail towards the ground.
CLUMPING Plants that grow into a compact thicket or mound.
ROSETTE Stems that fan out from a central point.

POSITION

Choosing where to place plants in our spaces is both an aesthetic and a functional decision. Plants are a wonderful way to enliven and soften a space, but some plants will work best in certain spots over others. Along with light requirements, allow a plant's shape to help communicate where it will really shine. Think about how big the plant may grow and what creative leaf textures and patterns you can combine for maximum (or minimal!) effect.

FLOOR Tall, upright plants that are often used to provide a focal point in a room look great in a large pot on the floor. Opt for mature specimens of *Strelitzia* and *Ficus*.

TABLETOP Low-lying and compact plants that sit perfectly on tables: think *Calathea* or *Peperomia*.

WINDOWSILL The bright, warm conditions of a windowsill work well for succulents and cacti that need lots of bright light and also enjoy direct morning sun. It's worth noting that true cacti species (non-jungle cacti, such as *Mammillaria* sp. and *Opuntia* sp.) need lots of direct sun – think large, unobstructed north-facing windows – to thrive.

BOOKSHELF OR STAND Cascading foliage from trailing plants, such as devil's ivy and hoyas, look fantastic on shelves and plant stands, where their trailing leaves soften harsh edges. Make use of the height to keep any toxic plants or cacti out of reach of pets and children.

COVERED BALCONY Hardier varieties and those that can withstand the elements (wind and even some direct sun) work well in sheltered outdoor spots. Agave as well as some begonias are good options.

TOXICITY

Many indoor plants have a level of toxicity when ingested by animals and humans alike, leading to symptoms from discomfort and vomiting through to more serious outcomes. Keep in mind that a lot of pets show zero interest in houseplants, but if you have a curious critter or just want to play it safe, opt for pet-friendly alternatives or keep them well out of reach of prying paws.

TOXIC Will cause significant harm if ingested.

MILDLY TOXIC May cause adverse reactions if ingested in large quantities.

PET FRIENDLY Perfectly safe for pets (and their owners).

Troubleshooting

Despite our best efforts to be good plant parents, when it comes to nature there are certain things that are beyond our control and sometimes plants get sick and die. It's a harsh reality, but it's also an important part of the journey of cultivating an indoor garden.

Caring for plants is often about experimentation and when things go wrong, rather than being discouraged, try and see each challenge as providing an opportunity to expand your knowledge. And don't forget to have realistic expectations. Imperfections are a part of life, so embrace the quirks, blemishes and irregularities.

When it comes to plant health, prevention is always best and checking in regularly with our foliage friends is the ideal way to nip any issues in the bud. The act of nurturing and maintaining our plants is an incredibly rewarding part of the process, and it's important to see it as such rather than viewing it as a chore. Take pleasure in watering and keeping foliage clean and healthy. Enjoy closely examining leaves and remove any sick or dead foliage, stems or flowers to prevent disease spreading to healthy parts of the plant. Your plants will inevitably thank you by looking their luscious best.

Observation, especially as you get to know the plants you bring into your collection, is vital for ensuring their light and water needs are being met. Plants are pretty good at communicating when they are unhappy, from leaf loss to browning tips. What's not so clear cut, however, is the underlying cause of your plant's symptoms. While sometimes it can be obvious (is your fragile forest floor–dwelling plant sitting in direct afternoon sun?), other issues, such as yellowing leaves, can be caused by both over- and under-watering so it can be a process of elimination to decipher what is going wrong. Opposite are explanations of what we commonly get wrong and how your plant is trying to tell you.

OVER- AND UNDER-WATERING Many plants have met an untimely death at the hands of an over-zealous plant parent who's been a little too eager with the watering can. Equally, long periods of drought can cause distress to many plants. Leaf drop, confusingly, can be a sign of both scenarios. It is vitally important to understand your plant's water needs and to always check the moisture level of the soil before watering. Ensure your pots have adequate drainage and that you empty run-off in a plant's saucer 30 minutes after you have watered.

Over-watering can lead to your plant's roots becoming waterlogged and rotten. The plant may appear dehydrated even though the soil is very wet. If your plant is suffering from root rot but seems salvageable, remove it from the soil and give the roots a good rinse. With a sharp pair of sanitised secateurs (avoid scissors), remove the affected roots. Depending on how much of the root system you need to remove, you may also need to remove one third to half of the foliage. Dipping the roots in a fungicide solution will kill off any fungus that may be present. Make sure you thoroughly wash the affected pot with disinfectant or diluted bleach to avoid spreading the fungus to the freshly potted plant.

Under-watered plants will often droop and leaves may curl in an effort to communicate their thirst. Additionally, dry, browning leaves or tips can be a sign that a plant is dehydrated. In these cases, the soil will be dry to the touch and the pot will be lighter than normal because of the lack of moisture.

DRY AIR FROM A HEATER OR COOLER Many indoor plants enjoy a warm, humid environment. Heating and air conditioning can cause the air in our homes to become incredibly dry, which, in turn, has a negative effect on foliage. Be sure to keep plants well away from direct hot or cold air; even a cold draught from a door or window is best avoided. A lack of adequate humidity will present as dry, brown leaf tips, and often comes with a side of pest infestation, such as spider mites.

LACK OF VENTILATION Prolonged damp conditions without good air circulation can allow fungi to thrive, leading to a variety of issues including root and stem rot, leaf spots and mildew. Circulating air from an open window or fan will decrease humidity and help the top layer of soil dry out between waterings.

OVER-FERTILISING Leaf burn that presents as browning tips can be an indication that a plant has been over-fertilised. Always follow product instructions and err on the side of caution when using fertiliser. It's much better to over-dilute than the other way around. Liquid fertiliser is always the best option for indoor plants, as it's easier to control application and prevent heavy handedness.

TOO MUCH OR TOO LITTLE LIGHT While older plant leaves may yellow and drop off as part of a plant's natural ageing process, leaves that become chlorotic (where leaves develop a yellow tinge all over because they produce insufficient chlorophyll) indicate that a plant is receiving too much light. Direct harsh afternoon sun can burn tropical foliage. While this damage is irreversible, it is mainly aesthetic and affected leaves can be removed to maintain the healthy appearance of the plant. Conversely, when exposed to low-light conditions plants may get 'leggy' with growth becoming sparse. Succulents are particularly susceptible to looking elongated if they don't have access to adequate light.

Pests + diseases

The more attentive you are to meeting your plants' needs, the less likely they are to succumb to pests or diseases.

Some problems, however, such as pests lying dormant in newly purchased potting mix, are unavoidable. It's important to keep an eye on any new plants that are brought into your fold and to regularly check in on your longer-standing pals, to get on top of any developing ailments before they fully take hold. Keep any new plants separate from your existing collection until you're sure they haven't brought in any unwanted guests. If you notice anything untoward on your existing plants, quarantine them until you're better able to identify the issue. Nursing a plant back to health after an infestation of mealy bug is incredibly satisfying, but it can be equally valuable to know when to call it quits with a plant for the sake of salvaging the others in your collection.

Again, it's vitally important to regularly check in on your plants and ensure all their water, light and humidity needs are being met. Pests and diseases most readily take hold of weak and unhealthy plants, so prevention is always preferable. When watering, be sure to remove any dead leaves or flowers, pinching or cutting them off at the base of the stem. This is also a great time to keep an eye out for any of the following telltale signs of pests and disease:

- Insects hanging out on the plant or in the potting mix.
- Brown spots, holes, webbing or nibbled leaf edges.
- Mold or powdery mildew.

There are lots of natural ways to control pests, and we always recommend using these over harsh chemicals. The most useful product we always have on hand is organic eco-oil or diluted vegetable oil, which acts as a natural insecticide to effectively suffocate pests (sorry, little dudes!), and has the added benefit of keeping your leaves looking nice and glossy. Either buy eco-oil in spray-bottle form, or dilute with water as per the product instructions and fill your own spray bottle to have at the ready.

Over the page you'll find a list of common pests and diseases and how to eradicate them.

APHIDS Small, soft-bodied, wingless insects that come in various colours. They reproduce rapidly and attack plants in clusters by sucking sap from the leaves and stems, causing physical damage and a metabolic imbalance. Outdoors, ladybugs are often used to manage aphids, but indoors use soapy water to wash the leaves and then apply eco-oil or vegetable oil.

FUNGUS GNATS Small flies that lay their eggs in potting mix. You may notice them running across the soil and leaves and crawling around on your windows. They are mainly just a nuisance as they do little damage. Make sure the affected plant is not over-watered and allow the top 5 cm (2 in) of soil to dry out. Use either sticky cards or a mixture of apple cider vinegar and dishwashing liquid (250 ml/1 cup vinegar and a few drops of dishwashing liquid) in a shallow dish to attract and trap these pesky gnats.

MEALYBUGS These bugs are not your friends. They are small insects coated in a white powdery wax that appear as small cotton wool–like clumps. They suck sap from leaves and excrete a sticky residue. They're often a little difficult to find as they're rather good at hiding, so be sure to check any new growth, plant joints and under leaves – basically any nooks and crannies on your plant. They thrive in over-fertilised, nitrogen-rich potting mix, so go easy there, soldier! It's best to use a balanced NPK (nitrogen–phosphorus–potassium) fertiliser on indoor plants to help keep nitrogen levels in check. To rid yourself of these little critters, physically remove them with a cloth, making sure they're squashed and not just displaced. Once you've removed all traces of them, spray the leaves (top and bottom), stems and potting mix with a mixture of one part vegetable oil with a dash of dishwashing liquid to 20 parts water (this mixture works great for scale too; see below). Repeat this spritz weekly for several weeks to ensure that all the bugs are gone.

SCALE Classified as either hard or soft, referring to the scales or 'outer shells' they exhibit, these flat- or oval-shaped slow-moving insects come in a variety of colours. Similar to mealybugs, scale suck plant juices and secrete honeydew, causing yellow, dropping leaves. Ants are a telltale sign that scale are nearby, as they love feeding on the sweet nectar. Rub off scale with an old toothbrush or a nail brush and then apply eco-oil. Wipe both sides of the leaves to smother any stragglers and remove any baby crawlers.

SPIDER MITES These teeny-tiny critters aren't actually true spiders, but rather members of the mite family. They are identified by small yellow or white dots or speckled patches, often found on the undersides of leaves. In cases of infestation, fine webbing may be visible. These little insects suck the life out of your plant so it's important to get on top of them quickly. Remove any badly infected leaves and discard them carefully so the mites can't find their way back or infect other plants. Wipe or shower down your plant, targeting the undersides of the leaves to remove any remaining mites. Spray the leaves with eco-oil to prevent any further outbreaks.

It's vitally important to regularly check in on your plants and ensure all their needs are being met. Pests and diseases most readily take hold of weak and unhealthy plants, so prevention is always preferable.

THRIPS These slender, winged insects are becoming an increasing issue for indoor gardeners. They suck the sap out of your plants and cause white- or silver-streaked damage, resulting in silver or brown leaves. You might also notice contorted growth and small brown fecal spots. Thrips can move from plant to plant pretty quickly, so it's best to tackle these pests as soon as you find them. Wipe or shower the leaves and then apply eco-oil or vegetable oil to the leaves, stems and potting mix.

WHITEFLIES Closely related to aphids, whiteflies look like delicate mini moths or flies. Adult whiteflies, along with their eggs, are often hidden on the undersides of leaves; if disturbed, the adults flutter off in a cloud. Like scale, they feed on a plant's juice and excrete honeydew causing stunted growth and yellow leaves. Whiteflies thrive in warm, humid environments, so if you live in a cooler climate you shouldn't have too much to worry about. To control whiteflies, gently vacuum them up or hose the insects away, before spraying the plant with eco-oil.

BACTERIA + VIRUSES These issues are usually caused by improper plant care. The most common causes are over- or under-watering, insufficient airflow, physical damage caused by ripping dead stems rather than cutting, and reusing old potting mix and dirty pots. Once established, bacteria and viruses can spread from plant to plant. They can stunt and distort plant growth and cause leaves to become discoloured or damaged. Generally, it is best to cut your losses and properly dispose of the plant before it infects others.

FUNGI Thriving in damp environments, fungi can cause root and stem rot, mildew and leaf spots. It can be pretty tricky to eliminate so, once again, prevention is key. Air circulation is your friend here, so regularly open those windows, turn on a fan and always allow the leaves and top layer of soil to dry out between watering. To treat fungi, isolate the plant, immediately apply an eco-fungicide and repeat as directed.

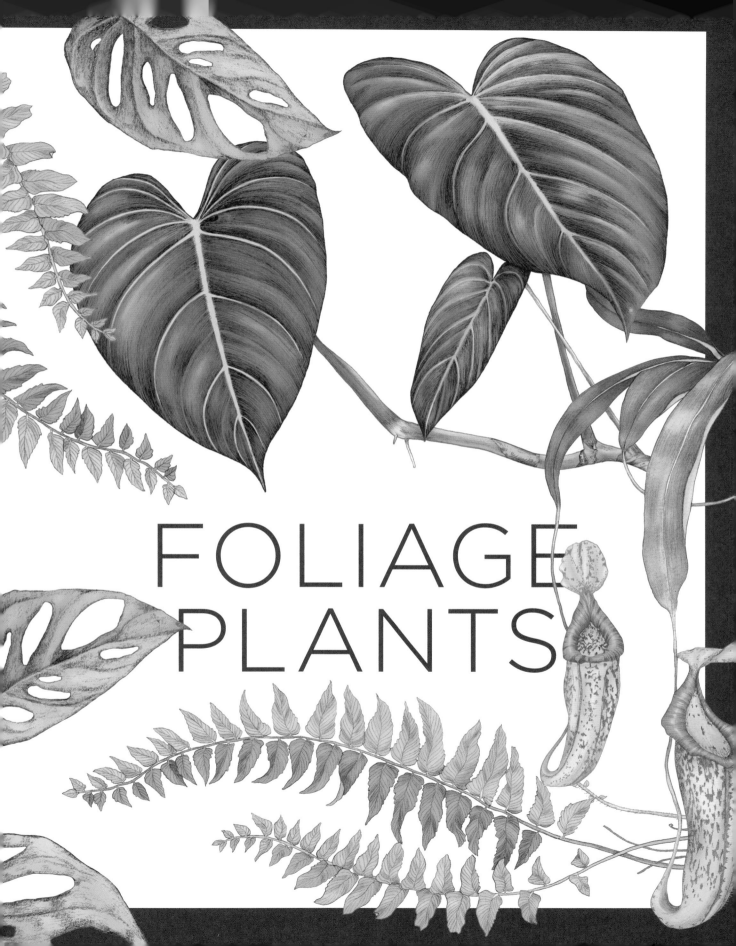

FOLIAGE PLANTS

Hoya

While many indoor plants are selected for their foliage alone, hoyas are the exception to the rule. A genus consisting of between 200 and 300 mostly tropical plants, many species are native to various parts of Asia, but are also found in the Philippines, Australia, New Guinea and Polynesia. They are celebrated as much for their clusters of sweet-smelling flowers as for their thick glossy leaves. These evergreen perennials are mainly vining (although some do take the form of woody shrubs), often growing epiphytically on trees in their natural environment.

While some varieties are considered succulents, most are not, even though they have fleshy leaves. Their foliage comes in a variety of shapes, colours and textures, from the curly cupped leaves of the *Hoya compacta* to the skinny, soft and slightly hairy leaves of the *Hoya linearis*. Popular in the 1970s and once regarded as plants only fit for Grandma's sitting room, appreciation for this generally easy-to-care-for genus has blossomed in recent times.

specimen *Hoya carnosa* × *serpens* 'Mathilde'

Hoya carnosa

COMMON NAME WAX PLANT

Probably the most readily available hoya, *Hoya carnosa* is native to Australia and Eastern Asia. It is sometimes unfavourably referred to as 'Grandma's old-fashioned wax plant', but you would be doing yourself a serious disservice to discount this delightfully chill houseplant.

CARE LEVEL
novice

LIGHT
bright, indirect

WATER
low–moderate

SOIL
well-draining

HUMIDITY
low

PROPAGATION
stem cuttings

GROWTH HABIT
trailing

POSITION
bookshelf or stand

TOXICITY
pet friendly

Trailing beautifully from a hanging pot or bookshelf, this unfussy hoya will grow happily in a very bright spot (important for encouraging flowers) with limited need for attention. Always water deeply but ensure that there is adequate drainage so the soil doesn't stay overly moist. Due to the robustness of its fleshy leaves, it will appreciate being left to dry out between waterings. If you're careful to keep the soil on the dry side during winter, you will be rewarded with some banging blooms come spring and summer. The wax plant's flowers are pretty balls of teeny tiny five-pointed stars, and they smell as sweet as they look.

As with most epiphytic hoyas, the wax plant likes its roots to be snug, so don't rush to repot. If doing so, ensure that the new pot is only slightly bigger than its current home. As with any plant, flowering expends a lot of its energy. In spring and summer, particularly when *Hoya carnosa* is in bloom, regular and consistent fertilising every couple of weeks is advised to help encourage strong growth.

Hoya carnosa × serpens 'Mathilde'

COMMON NAME HOYA MATHILDE

What do you get when you cross a *Hoya carnosa* with a *Hoya serpens*?
Why, the perfectly petite hoya Mathilde of course!

CARE LEVEL
novice

LIGHT
bright, indirect

WATER
low–moderate

SOIL
well-draining

HUMIDITY
low

PROPAGATION
stem cuttings

GROWTH HABIT
trailing

POSITION
bookshelf or stand

TOXICITY
pet friendly

This heavenly hybrid combines the best of both plants to create a compact and relatively easy-care hoya. It's near-round leaves, speckled with silver flecks (which are sometimes mistaken by hoya novices as disease or damage, but are actually highly prized!) trail beautifully from a hanging vessel or cascading from a shelf or sideboard. With the right conditions this hoya will flower early and often, delivering baby pink flowers that are gently fragranced and fuzzy in texture.

Although the Mathilde's foliage is glossy and fleshy, the plant is technically not a succulent and, as such, it should be potted in a well-aerated soil mix in a planter with drainage holes. Water deeply, but allow a good portion of the soil to dry out before watering again. To encourage the plant to flower, ensure that it has access to lots of bright, indirect light and keep the soil on the dry side in winter. Good news for pet lovers too, as the hoya Mathilde is non-toxic and thus safe for curious critters.

Hoya carnosa var. compacta

COMMON NAME INDIAN ROPE HOYA

The Indian rope hoya gets its common name from its draping vines of tight, curled leaves that resemble thick ropes. Its distinct appeal lies in that fleshy, contorted foliage, which is either dark green or variegated green and white.

CARE LEVEL
novice

LIGHT
bright, indirect

WATER
low–moderate

SOIL
well-draining

HUMIDITY
low

PROPAGATION
stem cuttings

GROWTH HABIT
trailing

POSITION
bookshelf or stand

TOXICITY
pet friendly

Although relatively slow growing, this hoya is a tough little plant that creates interest and curiosity in an indoor jungle.

As with other epiphytic hoyas, opt for a potting mix that is lightweight and provides both good drainage and excellent aeration. While the non-variegated *Hoya carnosa* var. *compacta* will tolerate lower-light conditions, growth will be further slowed and you will be unlikely to experience blooms. Bright, indirect light is, therefore, your best bet. In keeping with their low-maintenance vibe, these slow growers rarely need repotting, so choose a planter you love as it will be around for the long haul.

When the plant is in its active growing phase during spring and summer, allow the potting mix to almost fully dry out before watering again. During the cooler months, watering should be cut back even further, with the plant only requiring the occasional drink.

Hoya kerrii

COMMON NAME SWEETHEART HOYA

We're yet to meet a plant with heart-shaped leaves that we don't love and the *Hoya kerrii* is no exception.

CARE LEVEL
green thumb

LIGHT
bright, indirect

WATER
low–moderate

SOIL
well-draining

HUMIDITY
high

PROPAGATION
stem cuttings

GROWTH HABIT
climbing

POSITION
bookshelf or stand

TOXICITY
pet friendly

This hoya is often sold as a single-leaf cutting, especially around Valentine's Day, and while cute, these novelty leaves do not have all the necessary elements to grow into a plant. So, if a sea of hearts is more appealing, opt for a larger specimen (one sporting multiple leaves and nodes) or you'll be waiting a lifetime for this super-cute sweetheart to grow!

Native to Southeast Asia, in the wild this climber can grow up to 4 metres (13 ft) high. In a pot indoors it would take an exceptionally long time to reach such a size. Even if a stem and node are present, it can take several years before a vine grows, so patience is a virtue, but it's worth the wait. The silver lining is that it will rarely need to be repotted.

The succulent quality of the sweetheart hoya's foliage allows the plant to effectively store water, meaning you can wait longer between drinks than other hoyas. It makes for a hardy plant for the most part, but it does require a warm, humid climate to truly thrive. It will also appreciate a consistent watering schedule, along with reasonably bright light. It can even handle some direct morning rays.

Hoya linearis

COMMON NAME HOYA LINEARIS

Distinctly unique with delicate foliage that is elongated, soft and slightly hairy, *Hoya linearis* is not your average hoya. To us it is more reminiscent of a *Rhipsalis* (see page 379) or *Ceropegia linearis* (see page 337).

CARE LEVEL
green thumb

LIGHT
bright, indirect

WATER
moderate

SOIL
well-draining

HUMIDITY
low

PROPAGATION
stem cuttings

GROWTH HABIT
trailing

POSITION
bookshelf or stand

TOXICITY
pet friendly

While it may be a little harder to track down and care for than other hoyas, we think it's worth the effort for the incredible texture hoya linearis will bring to your plant gang. This epiphyte hails from in and around the Himalayan region of Northern India. Growing in the wild on trees at a high altitude, it prefers cooler temperatures compared to some other hoyas.

Without the more robust leaves of its relatives, the *Hoya linearis* is a little more demanding. While its care requirements are not dissimilar from other hoyas, it is less forgiving so establishing a consistent watering schedule is key. Ensure that the potting mix is aerated and well-draining, and that any excess water is removed from the saucer afterwards. The soil should be allowed to dry out between watering, but note that if the leaves are shrivelling, it probably needs a more regular drink. Very bright but generally indirect light is best, but as with other hoyas some gentle morning rays will be appreciated. In the right conditions you will enjoy white, star-shaped flowers with a slight scent of lemon.

Epipremnum

Epipremnum is a genus consisting of flowering evergreen perennial vines that climb with the aid of aerial roots. As such, it is not difficult to see why they are often confused with other genus within the Araceae family, such as *Rhaphidophora* and *Scindapsus*.

Found in tropical forests, from China and the base of the Himalayas, to Southeast Asia, Australia and the western Pacific Islands, these prolific growers reach heights of over 40 metres (131 ft), with leaves up to 3 metres (10 ft) long. Thankfully, you can lower your size expectations when growing *Epipremnum* in pots indoors; still, they make exceptionally stylish and resilient houseplants, meaning they're a great option for novices. They are not ideal, however, for those with plant-loving pets as all parts of the plants are toxic, mostly due to trichosclereids, small needle-like cells that help protect the plant from herbivores in the wild.

CARE LEVEL
novice

LIGHT
low-moderate

WATER
moderate

SOIL
well-draining

HUMIDITY
low

PROPAGATION
stem cuttings

GROWTH HABIT
trailing

POSITION
bookshelf or stand

TOXICITY
toxic

Epipremnum aureum

COMMON NAME DEVIL'S IVY

Indoor plants simply do not come more low maintenance and easy to grow than this handsome devil. Whether trailing, trained on hooks across a wall or creating a lush curtain of foliage, *Epipremnum aureum* makes a happy home in almost any space. Its common name, devil's ivy, is believed to have arisen due to it being almost impossible to kill – a characteristic that makes it a tremendous houseplant by anyone's standards. This fast-growing vine can grow to an astounding 20 metres (66 ft) long, with minimal effort on your part.

The resilience of this enduring vine means it is forgiving to those of us with a propensity for neglect. It will happily tolerate low light and can even withstand periods of drought. Having said that, try not to take advantage of its laidback nature. Bright, indirect light and a regular watering regime will allow the devil's ivy to thrive. Allow the top 2–5 cm (¾–2 in) of soil to dry out between drinks, as roots left in soggy potting mix will easily succumb to rot.

Propagation by stem cutting is easy: simply cut a stem with 5–7 leaves, cutting 2–3 cm (¾–1¼ in) below a leaf node. Remove the bottom leaves and place the stem in water. Once the roots have grown about 6 cm (2½ in), it is ready for planting in soil. Devil's ivy will also happily survive in water; just be sure to change it regularly.

Available in a variety of cultivars, from the common gold and green variegated golden devil's ivy to the light green neon pothos and the stylish white- and green-speckled marble queen, there's an *Epipremnum aureum* to satisfy everyone.

Epipremnum aureum
'marble queen'

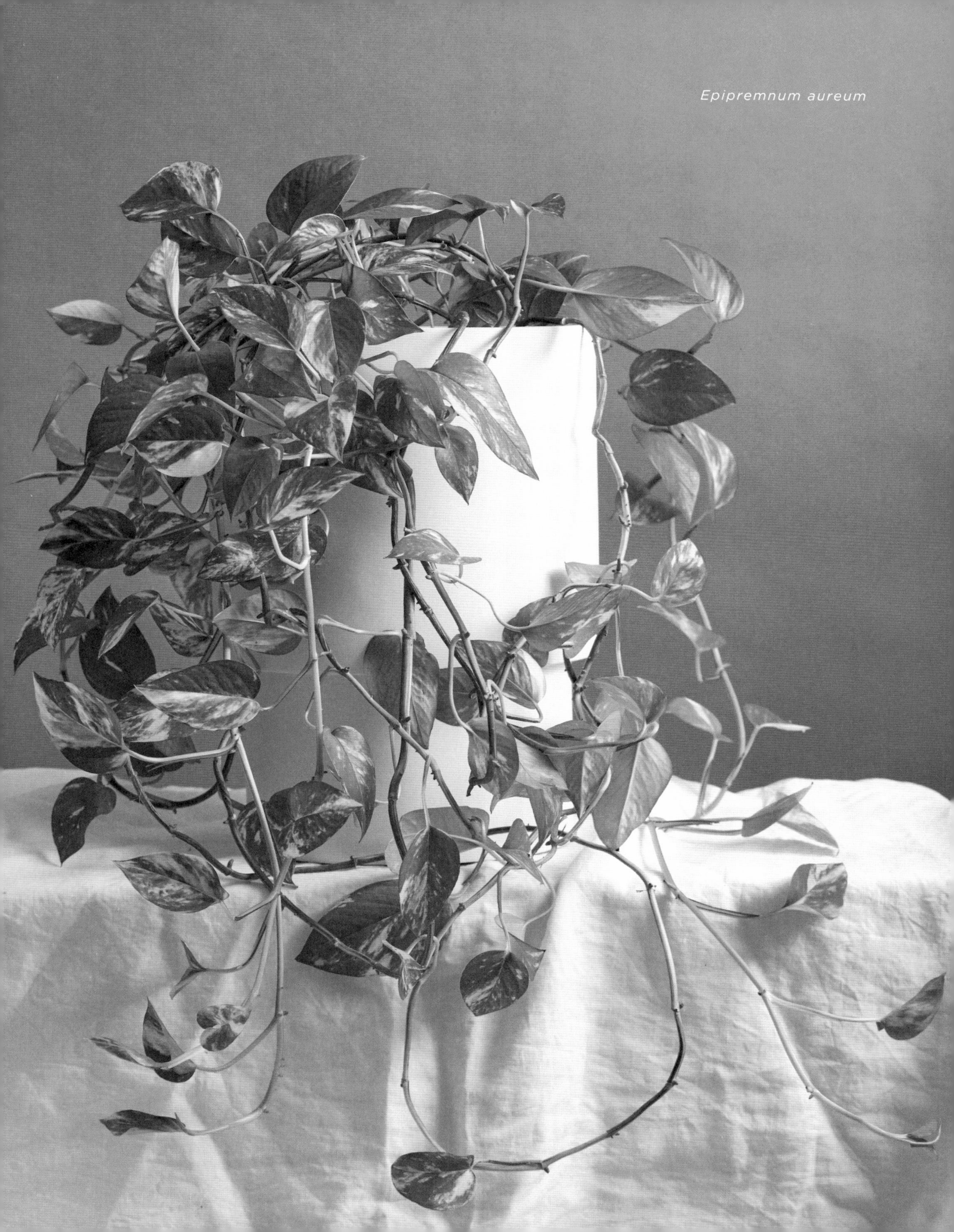
Epipremnum aureum

Pilea

With a name derived from the Latin word *pileus* meaning 'felt cap', due to the calyx covering the simple dry fruit the plants produce, *Pilea* is the largest genus of flowering plants in the nettle (Urticaceae) family. Made up of more than 600 species, these shade-loving herbs or shrubs thankfully lack the stinging hairs typical of the family. Found commonly throughout the tropics, subtropics and warm temperate regions, many *Pilea* make fabulous houseplants.

From the tiny, luminescent, silvery green leaves on the silver sprinkles (*Pilea sp.* 'NoID'; see page 62) to the metallic-splashed foliage of the aluminium plant (*Pilea cadierei*; see page 61), this pretty family of plants may be petite, but what they lack in size, they make up for with beautiful foliage and low-maintenance vibes.

Pilea cadierei

ALUMINIUM PLANT

Oval green leaves patterned with raised silvery splashes are the standout feature of the aluminium plant, which is surely the inspiration for its common name.

CARE LEVEL
novice

LIGHT
bright, indirect

WATER
moderate

SOIL
well-draining

HUMIDITY
medium

PROPAGATION
stem cuttings

GROWTH HABIT
upright

POSITION
tabletop

TOXICITY
toxic

This foliage, coupled with an easy-going nature and lack of any notable growing issues, sounds like the perfect indoor plant, and *Pilea cadierei* is just that. It is an excellent plant for gardeners of all levels and especially suited to small spaces.

In rare circumstances the aluminium plant does produce blooms, but they are small and inconsequential against the elaborately coloured leaves. If your plant does flower, you are best to pinch them off at the buds so the plant can expend the energy on producing more fabulous foliage instead. Pruning is important with

this *Pilea* and the stems should be trimmed back to half their length in the spring to encourage healthy, continued growth.

Short and sweet is the name of the game here. Generally, the aluminium plant has a lifespan of only about four years so make the most of this pretty plant while it's alive. At maximum height this diminutive indoor beauty will reach around 30 cm (12 in) in height, making it ideal for display on a tabletop or bench space. If space is truly at a premium, the dwarf cultivar *Pilea cadierei* 'minima' tops out at around 15 cm (6 in) with half-sized leaves.

Pilea sp. 'NoID'

COMMON NAME SILVER SPRINKLES

Perfectly described by its common name silver sprinkles, this *Pilea* is a delightfully petite trailing plant that appears to glimmer as though its leaves have been scattered with fairy dust.

CARE LEVEL
novice

LIGHT
bright, indirect

WATER
low–moderate

SOIL
well-draining

HUMIDITY
medium

PROPAGATION
stem cuttings

GROWTH HABIT
trailing

POSITION
bookshelf or stand

TOXICITY
pet friendly

This *Pilea* is somewhat of a curiosity in that it appears to have made it into trade before being botanically described, published and, therefore, accepted. As such, even though it is often called *Pilea libanensis*, it technically has no botanical name. Further complicating matters is the fact that silver sprinkles is often labelled by nurseries and garden centres as 'Pilea glauca', a name purely created for trade and not to be confused with the species *Pilea glauco-phylla*. If you're trying to track one down, be on the lookout for either names, but know that neither is theoretically correct.

Semantics aside, this *Pilea* is a delightfully easy-care plant. Bright, indirect light is best and while it will tolerate lower-light conditions it is less forgiving of a full sun position. The silver sprinkles will thrive in high humidity, so regular misting is advised but it will also cope with a less humid clime without too much fuss. Good drainage is essential to avoid root rot. To help, add perlite to the potting mix and be sure to let the top 5 cm (2 in) of soil dry out between watering. On the other hand, those miniature leaves will dry and brown if subjected to periods of drought, so it's important to strike the right balance.

A hanging planter makes a good home for the silver sprinkles or it looks equally good trailing from a shelf. Pinch back the stems when needed to help thicken up the plant and encourage fresh new growth.

Pilea peperomioides

COMMON NAME CHINESE MONEY PLANT

Not so long ago, the Chinese money plant was a hot commodity. A regular feature in Scandinavian interiors, their big, round, glossy leaves sprawling out on long thin stems make for a striking indoor plant, and their initial elusiveness only adds to their appeal.

CARE LEVEL
novice

LIGHT
bright, indirect

WATER
moderate

SOIL
well-draining

HUMIDITY
medium

PROPAGATION
offsets + plantlets

GROWTH HABIT
clumping

POSITION
tabletop

TOXICITY
pet friendly

While their popularity hasn't waned, the Chinese money plant is now far easier to acquire, which is great news as they make a fantastic addition to an indoor jungle. Also known as the friendship plant, missionary plant, pancake plant, UFO plant or just pilea, the *Pilea peperomioides* originates from the southwestern Yunnan province of China.

The plant has a lovely backstory that explains the origin of some of its common names. The story goes that a Norwegian missionary in China took cuttings home with him in the 1940s, to share with friends and family. They fast spread throughout Scandinavia and beyond, as cuttings were passed between more and more communities. This continued for decades with the species still unknown in Europe, until the early 1970s when the houseplant trend was peaking and people became increasingly interested to find out what it was.

Specimens of the plant were sent to London's Kew Gardens, but without any flowers, identification eluded botanists.

Eventually, in 1978, after much public noise, someone sent in leaves along with a male flowering inflorescence. One Kew botanist suggested that it 'could be *Pilea peperomioides*...', and he wasn't wrong. The mystery had been solved.

Producing pups or mini versions of itself, the *Pilea peperomioides* can be easily propagated by separating the pups from the mother plant at the roots (with a very sharp knife or secateurs) and allowing them to root in water or moist potting mix. As the history of the plant suggests, gifting these pups is a lovely way to spread some plant love.

In the right conditions, this *Pilea* is a wonderfully low-maintenance housemate. A position with lots of bright, indirect light and access to some direct morning sun will allow it to thrive. Water deeply, soaking the soil and allowing any excess to drain from the base of the planter, then ensure the top 5 cm (2 in) of soil is dry before watering again. Misting the leaves will be appreciated but this is not essential so you can suit yourself.

Syngonium

Native to tropical rainforests in Central and South America, Mexico and the West Indies, these humble plants are a stalwart of the house-plant game. Most *Syngonium* are cultivars and are often extremely variable when it comes to colouration and patterning. The leaves can range from dark to neon green and brown to pink (such as the *Syngonium podophyllum* 'neon robusta'), while others are almost all white (we're looking at you *Syngonium* 'moonshine'), or mottled like one of our favourites, the variegated *Syngonium podophyllum* 'albo variegatum'. With their vibrant leaves, semi-mature *Syngonoum* can be easily mis-taken for a type of *Caladium*.

Junior plants generally start out with petite heart-shaped leaves, becoming more arrow shaped and finally lobed when fully mature. When young, the plants grow in a bushy habit, and will send out vines as they mature. It's up to you whether to prune the vines and keep them compact, or let them branch out, so to speak. A number of species, including *S. angustatum,* are invasive in some areas, so always do your research before planting any *Syngonium* outside.

CARE LEVEL
novice

LIGHT
bright, indirect

WATER
moderate

SOIL
well-draining

HUMIDITY
medium

PROPAGATION
stem cuttings

GROWTH HABIT
climbing + trailing

POSITION
bookshelf or stand

TOXICITY
toxic

Syngonium podophyllum

COMMON NAME **ARROWHEAD VINE**

Syngonium podophyllum is the most commonly cultivated *Syngonium* species. Native to the tropical and subtropical climes of many countries, from Mexico trailing down to Bolivia, this plant grows very happily indoors. It is a prolific grower with leaves that become larger and more arrow shaped as the plant ages. Lobes will appear as the plant reaches full maturity. Clumping at first, the arrowhead vine will want to climb once it gets settled, so either prune (and propagate!) if you'd like to keep your plant small, or place it on a shelf or insert a totem pole if you'd like to see it change shape.

Broadly speaking, all *S. podophyllum* cultivars are great plants for beginners as they're pretty unfussy and tolerant of some neglect. While those with darker leaves will endure lower-light conditions, generally these plants will thrive in bright, indirect light. Those with variegation, like the cultivar *Syngonium podophyllum* 'albo variegatum', will need a good amount of bright light to maintain their desirable white marbling (as with all variegated species), but keep them away from harsh, direct sunrays.

These plants often grow in semi-aquatic environments in the wild and, as such, can handle higher moisture levels, but moderate watering will still be best, ensuring that they don't end up sitting in a saucer filled with water for long. Their aquatic nature also means they propagate easily in water – stem cuttings should root within a matter of weeks. The arrowhead vine will benefit from semi-regular leaf misting and a dose of half-strength fortnightly fertiliser in the warmer months.

Syngonium podophyllum
'albo variegatum'

specimen *Monstera adansonii*

Monstera

With a name derived from the Latin word for monstrous or abnormal, *Monstera* is a genus of about 50 flowering plants sporting unusual and spectacular foliage, often punctuated by naturally occurring holes or fenestrations. Members of the Arum or Araceae family and native to the tropical regions of the Americas, these evergreen vines make marvellous houseplants.

Monstera deliciosa (Swiss cheese plant) is without doubt the best-known representative of the genus and the most widely found in homes worldwide, but harder-to-find species, such as *Monstera adansonii*, are fast becoming favourites with indoor gardeners. While in the wild these botanical beasts can reach heights of 20 metres (60 ft), scaling large trees by means of aerial roots, they are unlikely to get this big indoors.

As with other members of the Araceae family, monsteras produce a specialised inflorescence called a spadix, which is a spike of minute flowers tightly clustered together. While you are unlikely to experience this on indoor specimens, rest assured the foliage alone makes this genus worthy of prime position in your indoor jungle.

Monstera adansonii

SWISS CHEESE VINE

Daintier but no less dazzling than *Monstera deliciosa* is the *Monstera adansonii*, with its heart-shaped foliage perforated by the graphic holes synonymous with this genus.

CARE LEVEL
green thumb

LIGHT
bright, indirect

WATER
moderate–high

SOIL
well-draining

HUMIDITY
high

PROPAGATION
stem cuttings

GROWTH HABIT
climbing + trailing

POSITION
bookshelf or stand

TOXICITY
toxic

Native to Central and South America, the Swiss cheese vine is often confused with *Monstera obliqua* which, with its slimmer leaves and bigger holes, is far more rare and elusive than *M. adansonii*.

Bright, indirect light conditions are best for this vine, and be sure to keep the potting mix consistently moist but never soggy. A well-draining potting mix with added coco coir will retain moisture while ensuring the plant doesn't get waterlogged. These jungle dwellers crave high humidity, which can be lacking in our homes. Regular misting is advised and if you're really serious, a humidifier would be ideal. A lack of nutritious soil won't go unnoticed by the Swiss cheese vine so

you will do well to refresh its potting mix annually. Additionally, look to feed with half-strength fertiliser every few weeks during the growing seasons.

This versatile *Monstera* can be trained across a wall with small hooks, staked for more upright growth or allowed to cascade from a hanging planter. But note that without adequate support it does have a tendency to get leggy with reduced foliage size. This vining beauty appreciates a solid textured totem to attach to, and will reward you with larger, fuller growth. It propagates well from stem cuttings, which can be planted back into the pot of the original plant to help thicken up the foliage.

Monstera deliciosa

COMMON NAME **SWISS CHEESE PLANT**

An absolute stalwart of the indoor plant world, you're sure to find a *Monstera deliciosa* in the collection of any indoor gardener worth their salt. A tropical beauty hailing from parts of southern Mexico through to southern Panama, it makes a graphic and decidedly lush statement in any space.

CARE LEVEL
novice

LIGHT
bright, indirect

WATER
moderate

SOIL
well-draining

HUMIDITY
medium

PROPAGATION
stem cuttings

GROWTH HABIT
climbing

POSITION
floor + stand

TOXICITY
toxic

Its solid, heart-shaped juvenile leaves are beautiful in their own right, but it's as the plant matures that those fabulous fenestrations for which the Swiss cheese plant is known come into their own.

Apart from its good looks, this plant is one low-maintenance monster. In a spot enjoying bright, indirect light and with a consistent watering schedule (allowing the top 5 cm/2 in of soil to dry out in between drinks), *Monstera deliciosa* will flourish. Be sure to give it room to grow as these guys get big, fast. A solid stake is useful for wrangling the Swiss cheese plant, giving it much-needed support on which to climb.

It can be propagated in water or potting mix from a stem cutting that includes a leaf node and aerial root, which is good to know for when your plant requires taming or outgrows its home.

While its Latin name is derived from the 'delicious' fruit the plant bears in the wild, which is said to taste like a fruit salad, indoor conditions rarely promote fruit development. It's no great loss, though, when you have those glorious leaves to admire. Be sure to keep the large surface area of the leaves dust free with a regular wipe down or a shower every now and then. Misting will also be appreciated.

Monstera deliciosa 'borsigiana variegata'

COMMON NAME VARIEGATED SWISS CHEESE PLANT

Sometimes a plant becomes a hot-ticket item, and this is certainly the case with this lusted-after variegated *Monstera*.

CARE LEVEL
green thumb

LIGHT
bright, indirect

WATER
moderate

SOIL
well-draining

HUMIDITY
high

PROPAGATION
stem cuttings

GROWTH HABIT
climbing

POSITION
floor

TOXICITY
toxic

Pictured here is the magnificent *Monstera deliciosa* 'borsigiana variegata'. Admired for its unique variegated effect, this unicorn is one of the most highly sought-after plants of recent years, and it's not hard to see why. Those incredible leaves, which look as though they've been painted, can grow up to nearly one metre (3 ft, 3 in) wide and, like the regular *M. deliciosa*, develop large holes as the plant matures. Each leaf is unique with exceptionally beautiful cream and green patterning.

As with all variegated plants, the *M. deliciosa* 'borsigiana variegata' requires a super bright position. The non-green areas of foliage are unable to absorb light, meaning the plant has to work twice as hard to photosynthesise. Be sure to keep that light indirect, however, as harsh sun will burn its stunning foliage. It grows more slowly than its green counterpart, but can reach the same lofty heights, so ensure that it has plenty of room to spread its wings. It is also less tolerant of periods of drought than the non-variegated Swiss cheese plant; the soil should be kept moist but not soggy, so adequate drainage is key.

Browning edges, particularly on the creamy sections of leaves, are not uncommon and could be a result of low humidity, insufficient watering or sun damage. If you really want to treat this beauty (that you probably spent a decent amount of money on), then distilled or rain water is the way to go.

In addition to the 'borsigiana variegata', other variegated *Monstera* in circulation include the *M. deliciosa* var. borsigiana 'aurea variegata', *M. deliciosa* 'Thai constellation' and the scarcest of the lot, *M. deliciosa* var. *albo variegata*, an exceptionally slow-growing and rare beast indeed.

Monstera siltepecana

COMMON NAME **SILVER LEAF MONSTERA**

Another of the more elusive monsteras, *Monstera siltepecana* hails from Mexico and many parts of Central America.

CARE LEVEL
novice

LIGHT
bright, indirect

WATER
moderate

SOIL
well-draining

HUMIDITY
high

PROPAGATION
stem cuttings

GROWTH HABIT
climbing + trailing

POSITION
bookshelf or stand

TOXICITY
toxic

If you can get your hands on this tropical vine you will be rewarded with a fast-growing, easy-to-care-for houseplant with some serious good looks. In the wild, as it matures from a terrestrial juvenile plant to an epiphytic vining beauty, its silvery leaves, with distinct deep green veins, turn dark green and develop the same fenestrations for which the *Monstera* genus is so adored.

This rainforest dweller appreciates lots of bright, indirect light, consistently moist soil and high humidity when kept indoors. When its needs are adequately met it is an incredibly fast grower, but it will generally remain in its juvenile form in home cultivation. Much like *M. adansonii*, the silver leaf monstera works equally well trailing from a hanging planter or cascading from a shelf or plant stand. They are also popular for use in terrariums.

If the vines of your *M. siltepecana* start to become unruly they can be trimmed and easily propagated to create more plants. With this special monstera hard to come by, you'll have fellow plant lovers lined up at your door for a cutting.

Calathea + Goeppertia

The genus *Goeppertia* has long been contested in the scientific community, with many plants reclassified to the closely related genus *Calathea*. A series of genetic tests undertaken circa 2012, however, revealed that one of the subgenera of *Calathea* had, in fact, a different ancestor and, as such, the *Goeppertia* genus was revived and 250 species were reclassified back. Confusingly, many people, and even nurseries, still refer to these plants as *Calathea* and so for ease we have grouped these two genera together.

Whichever plants you choose to seek out, the incredible watercolour-esque patterns on the leaves of *Calathea* or *Geoppertia* make them highly recognisable and hugely sought after. The way their leaves rise and fall, as if dancing, over the course of the day is a sight to behold and the reason they are commonly referred to as prayer plants. Native to the tropical Americas, sadly several species are threatened by extinction in the wild, serving as a reminder of the delicate nature of our ecosystems and our responsibility to protect them in any way we can.

Calathea lietzei

COMMON NAME PEACOCK PLANT

The *Calathea lietzei* and its cultivars are truly striking, but in return they require some special attention.

CARE LEVEL
green thumb

LIGHT
bright, indirect

WATER
moderate

SOIL
well-draining

HUMIDITY
high

PROPAGATION
division

GROWTH HABIT
clumping

POSITION
tabletop

TOXICITY
pet friendly

For this Latin American beauty, high humidity goes with the territory and anything less will result in brown edges marring that fabulous foliage. If you're really serious, investing in a humidifier is your best bet, but frequent misting and sitting your plant on a water-filled pebble tray is the next best thing.

Featured here is the most common cultivar, *C. lietzei* 'white fusion', whose leaves look as if they have been painted by a master, with strokes of white and light and dark green, and purple-pink undersides.

The peacock plant can handle slightly lower-light conditions, but to maintain the variegation for which this plant is so adored, ensure it receives bright, indirect light avoiding direct sun. Keep the soil consistently moist, watering when just the top layer has dried out; conversely, be sure to avoid overwatering. It's all about getting the balance right, which you will learn as you get to know your plant.

Although more fickle than other calatheas, the white fusion can bounce back from a little mistreatment. Simply remove damaged leaves and return it to a regular watering and misting schedule.

Goeppertia kegeljanii

NETWORK CALATHEA syn: *Calathea musaica*

Described by some as reminiscent of a woven tapestry or a stained-glass mosaic, an intricate series of stripes attractively adorn the bright green leaves of the network calathea.

CARE LEVEL
green thumb

LIGHT
bright, indirect

WATER
moderate

SOIL
well-draining

HUMIDITY
low

PROPAGATION
division

GROWTH HABIT
upright

POSITION
tabletop

TOXICITY
pet friendly

Whatever you see when you look into these leaves, the matrix of patterns is seriously stunning.

Hailing from the rainforests of Brazil, this is by far the toughest species within the *Goeppertia* genus. Unlike its cousins, the network calathea doesn't demand high humidity, so there's no need to stress if you don't get to spritzing it every day. They are also less prone to spider mites that can ravage the moisture-hungry species. Because of its waxy, moisture-retaining leaves, it is also tolerant of brighter light conditions than some, and it will benefit from some gentle morning light, but avoid harsh afternoon rays. Water moderately, allowing the top 5 cm (2 in) of soil to dry out before watering again.

Repot your *G. kegeljanii* every one to two years in spring. This is also a great time to divide your plant and propagate new ones. We recommend placing your *Calathea* and *Goeppertia* together – it not only makes a big visual impact with their different patterns bustling for attention, but it also helps to maintain humidity levels and allows you to easily check on your plants in one hit.

Goeppertia orbifolia

COMMON NAME **PEACOCK PLANT** syn: *Calathea orbifolia*

Large, bright green foliage with silver stripes that increase in size with each new leaf, the *Goeppertia orbifolia* is a true show-off, just like its namesake bird, the peacock.

CARE LEVEL
green thumb

LIGHT
low–moderate

WATER
moderate

SOIL
moisture-retaining

HUMIDITY
high

PROPAGATION
division

GROWTH HABIT
clumping

POSITION
tabletop

TOXICITY
pet friendly

We love it for these striking leaves and the fresh, graphic vibe it brings to any indoor jungle, but keep in mind that these good looks don't necessarily come easily. This diva demands high humidity akin to the levels it's used to in its natural habitat, and it's safe to say that this is the most crucial care factor for this plant. Be sure to keep it clear of cold draughts and air-conditioning units, and close to a source of humidity whether that be your trusty mister, a pebble tray filled with water and/or grouped with lots of other humidity-loving plant pals.

Hailing from the forest floor, this gorgeous plant is tolerant of lower-light conditions, but it will thrive in bright, indirect sunlight. Direct sun, particularly later in the day, will burn and damage this calathea's foliage and should be avoided. Use filtered water where possible and be sure to keep the soil relatively moist but never soggy. Always remove any excess water from saucers shortly after watering. Fertilise every fortnight with a half-strength liquid fertiliser during spring and summer, and use a damp cloth to wipe the leaves clean. In general, we suggest avoiding shine sprays, but particularly in this instance as the foliage is sensitive. Instead, opt for horticultural oil or eco-oil for the same glossy result without the nasties.

Goeppertia orbifolia can be propagated every couple of years. In spring, gently divide the root system into two plants and then immediately repot both into fresh potting mix. Soon enough you'll have grown a peacock plant for every room.

Philodendron

The second largest genus within the Araceae family, *Philodendron* is made up of almost 500 plants, many of which are fabulously at home indoors. With a name derived from the Greek words for love (philo) and tree (dendron), it is very easy to fall for this varied but undoubtedly lush group of plants. As with all members of the Araceae family, philodendrons are leafy tropical plants that reproduce by forming clusters of many tiny flowers that grow on a spike-like structure called a spadix, sheathed by a modified leaf called a spathe. Their growth methods are diverse, but many philodendrons begin life as terrestrial plants on the forest floor and then transform into epiphytes as they climb upwards.

The juvenile leaves of most philodendrons differ dramatically from their mature foliage, but both can be appreciated. From the rich, velvety leaves of *P. hederaceum* var. *hederaceum* (see page 102) to the epic white-veined foliage of *P. gloriosum* (see page 105), these tropical plants are sure to add colour, texture and spectacle to your indoor jungle at any stage.

specimen *Philodendron melanochrysum* × *gloriosum* 'glorious'

Philodendron bipennifolium

COMMON NAME HORSEHEAD PHILODENDRON

If you're looking for a philodendron a little out of leftfield, look no further than *Philodendron bipennifolium*. Large, fiddle-shaped leaves that are glossy and green are what gives the horsehead or fiddle-leaf philodendron its common moniker.

CARE LEVEL
novice

LIGHT
bright, indirect

WATER
moderate

SOIL
well-draining

HUMIDITY
medium

PROPAGATION
stem cuttings

GROWTH HABIT
climbing

POSITION
bookshelf or stand

TOXICITY
toxic

This plant is known as a hemi-epiphyte, meaning it starts life in the soil before attaching to a tree and climbing towards the top of the rainforest canopy with the assistance of its long stem and aerial roots. It is for this reason that this fast-growing tropical plant does best when supported by a solid stake or totem.

Originating in the tropical rainforests of southern Brazil, Argentina and Bolivia, horsehead philodendrons require bright, indirect light to thrive. Always water deeply, allowing the excess to drain away and then wait until the top 5 cm (2 in) of soil is dry before watering again. Keeping the large foliage dust free facilitates good photosynthesis and keeps this houseplant happy. Repotting every couple of years to refresh the soil is recommended, but you won't need to increase the pot size each time as these guys like to be snug in their container. As with all philodendrons, they are considered toxic so keep away from pets and small children.

Philodendron 'birkin'

COMMON NAME PHILODENDRON BIRKIN

Champagne taste on a beer budget? Designer handbags go out of fashion, but this birkin will endure and won't break the bank.

CARE LEVEL
novice

LIGHT
bright, indirect

WATER
moderate

SOIL
well-draining

HUMIDITY
low

PROPAGATION
stem cuttings

GROWTH HABIT
trailing

POSITION
bookshelf or stand

TOXICITY
toxic

With deep green foliage patterned with pinstripes of creamy white, this stylish and highly sought-after houseplant will add serious panache to your indoor jungle. It is a relatively new hybrid and, as such, there is some conjecture about its height at maturity, with sources ranging from 50–100 cm (1½–3 ft, 3 in). Either way, it's a slow-growing and beautifully compact philodendron.

Like most plants within the genus, the birkin is pretty low maintenance. Bright, indirect light is important for maintaining the strong variegation of its foliage, and a well-draining potting mix that is sufficiently aerated is best. *P. birkin* can tolerate drier conditions, and will thrive in the low humidity of many indoor environments. During spring and summer, fertilise regularly to promote fresh growth.

Philodendron erubescens 'white princess'

COMMON NAME WHITE PRINCESS PHILODENDRON

There's no need to curtsy for this royal subject, but you may not be able to help yourself as the *Philodendron erubescens* 'white princess' delights with some truly regal foliage.

CARE LEVEL
novice

LIGHT
bright, indirect

WATER
moderate

SOIL
well-draining

HUMIDITY
medium

PROPAGATION
division

GROWTH HABIT
clumping + trailing

POSITION
tabletop

TOXICITY
toxic

The large green leaves of this Colombian native are splashed with white variegation that makes a beautiful statement among a sea of greenery. Although relatively slow growing, as the plant matures you can stake it to encourage upright growth or allow it to eventually trail. For royalty, this princess is decidedly low maintenance, but be sure to provide plenty of bright, indirect light to sustain the beautiful leaf patterning for which this philodendron is so well loved.

Water moderately, allowing the top 5 cm (2 in) of well-draining potting mix to dry out between drinks, but keep humidity relatively high where possible.

Regular misting or sitting the plant over water in a pebble-filled saucer will be appreciated. *Philodendron erubescens* will not tolerate the cold, so protect from frost and dramatic changes in temperature. To keep foliage flourishing, be sure to keep the leaves dust free, wiping them regularly with a damp cloth and rinsing in the shower once a month or so.

Looking for something with a little more colour? Fans of the white princess philodendron will fall just as hard for the pink princess and prince of orange, which, as their names suggest, provide vibrant colour to any indoor jungle.

Philodendron erubescens
'prince of orange'

Philodendron hederaceum

COMMON NAME HEARTLEAF PHILODENDRON

With the most stunning heart-shaped leaves, it's sure to be love at first sight with this little sweetheart.

CARE LEVEL
novice

LIGHT
bright, indirect

WATER
moderate

SOIL
well-draining

HUMIDITY
medium

PROPAGATION
stem cuttings +
division

GROWTH HABIT
climbing + trailing

POSITION
bookshelf or stand

TOXICITY
toxic

Philodendron hederaceum is a hemi-epiphyte that makes a stunning climbing and trailing plant. It perfectly softens a bookshelf with its cascading green foliage, but is equally happy growing upwards with support. Exceptionally low maintenance, nothing fancy is required to court the heartleaf philodendron, and in return you'll get some of the loveliest leaves that will keep your air free from toxins, such as formaldehyde and benzene.

Forgetful plant parents can rest easy as this relaxed philodendron will take a little neglect in its stride. Bright, indirect light is ideal but it will tolerate lower light like a champ. It can also handle short dry periods, but it will enjoy a regular deep water once the top 5 cm (2 in) of soil has dried out. Keep your *P. hederaceum* neat and tidy with regular pruning, which will also help to thicken up growth. Stem cuttings propagate easily in water so you can share the love and gift this sweet gal on to friends and family. As with all philodendrons the heartleaf is toxic, so keep away from paws and small fingers.

Philodendron hederaceum 'Brasil'

COMMON NAME PHILODENDRON 'BRASIL'

If you thought leaves didn't come sweeter than the heartleaf philodendron on page 98 then think again. For a colourful twist on the classic, look no further than the striking philodendron 'Brasil'.

CARE LEVEL
novice

LIGHT
bright, indirect

WATER
moderate

SOIL
well-draining

HUMIDITY
medium

PROPAGATION
stem cuttings

GROWTH HABIT
trailing + climbing

POSITION
bookshelf or stand

TOXICITY
toxic

With foliage that appears painted with the colours of the Brazilian flag, and some seriously low-maintenance vibes, this is one heck of a houseplant for even the most novice of plant parents.

The care requirements for this philodendron are not dissimilar to that of its green counterpart. It, too, will tolerate a wide range of light conditions, but to ensure the variegated foliage (which is surely the reason you bought it in the first place) is retained, you will need to supply plenty of bright, indirect light. In optimum conditions this plant is a prolific grower, producing long cascading vines that will be reaching the floor in no time. Let it trail happily from a shelf or hanging planter, pinching back stems (by gently pruning just above a node) near the top of the plant to encourage thicker growth.

The philodendron 'Brasil' has moderate water needs: a good soaking roughly once a week should do the trick, allowing the top 2–5 cm (¾–2 in) of soil to dry out between watering. While it's always best to establish a consistent watering schedule, neglectful gardeners can rest easy with this magnanimous houseplant.

Philodendron hederaceum var. *hederaceum*

COMMON NAME VELVET LEAF PHILODENDRON

Rich, bronze heart-shaped leaves suspend elegantly from this vining philodendron. They unfurl reddy-coppery in colour, hardening to an iridescent, dark emerald green with a red tint.

CARE LEVEL
novice

LIGHT
bright, indirect

WATER
high

SOIL
well-draining

HUMIDITY
high

PROPAGATION
stem cuttings

GROWTH HABIT
climbing + trailing

POSITION
bookshelf or stand

TOXICITY
toxic

In addition, the leaves are thin enough to appear translucent and almost metallic as the light shines through. It is this textural quality that inspires its common name and ensures that this is no ordinary plant.

Thankfully, these good looks don't equal high maintenance. The velvet leaf philodendron will thrive in bright, indirect light but it can also cope with lower-light situations. In the warmer months, keep the soil consistently moist, watering only when the top layer of soil is dry. Water less in autumn and winter when growth is slowed.

The velvet leaf philodendron is often incorrectly called *Philodendron* 'micans' or *Philodendron hederaceum* 'micans', perhaps because its actual name is a little more complicated. Names aside, however, it will delight whether trained up a stake or across a wall, or allowed to trail freely. If those vines get too long and unruly, simply trim them back and propagate any stem cuttings in water before replanting or gifting. Not a fan of the cold, this philodendron will often become winter-deciduous in cooler climates.

Philodendron melanochrysum × gloriosum 'glorious'

COMMON NAME **PHILODENDRON 'GLORIOUS'**

This relatively rare aroid is highly sought after and for good reason. With the right care it makes a fantastic houseplant.

CARE LEVEL
green thumb

LIGHT
bright, indirect

WATER
high

SOIL
well-draining

HUMIDITY
high

PROPAGATION
stem cuttings

GROWTH HABIT
climbing

POSITION
bookshelf or stand

TOXICITY
toxic

It's all in the name of this glorious philodendron. Foliage certainly doesn't come more sumptuous than the glimmering velvety leaves of this stunning hybrid of *Philodendron gloriosum* and *P. melanochrysum*, created by Keith Henderson in the 1970s. Graphic white veining intersects the rich green on the large textured leaves of this much sought-after aroid.

The philodendron 'glorious' should be potted in a well-draining soil mix and kept consistently moist but never soggy. Its humidity requirements are also high, so regular misting is advised. As with all philodendrons, bright indirect light is best, so avoid direct sun, which will burn those lovely leaves. A moss-covered pole makes the ideal totem for this vining houseplant, providing support for strong upright growth if that's your vibe.

Philodendron pedatum

COMMON NAME OAK LEAF PHILODENDRON

If large-leafed climbers are your jam then look no further than the oak leaf philodendron.

CARE LEVEL
novice

LIGHT
bright, indirect

WATER
moderate

SOIL
well-draining

HUMIDITY
medium

PROPAGATION
stem cuttings

GROWTH HABIT
climbing

POSITION
floor

TOXICITY
toxic

Native to Brazil and Venezuela, the *Philodendron pedatum*'s leaves, as the common name suggests, are similarly shaped to an oak leaf. Featuring multiple lobes, they are glossy and lush with deep ridges that add texture and interest. As with all vining philodendrons, this houseplant needs space and support to climb, but treat this baby right and you could end up with foliage over 30 cm (12 in) long!

This houseplant is low-maintenance and perfect for indoor gardeners of all levels. Plant in a well-draining, aerated potting mix and water deeply once the top 5 cm (2 in) of soil has dried out. While this easy-going philodendron will tolerate a range of conditions, a position with plenty of bright, indirect light is best. To promote rapid growth, fertilise monthly in spring and summer, and wipe the leaves from time to time to avoid dust build-up.

Philodendron sodiroi ×
Philodendron verrucosum
While the creator of this exceptional hybrid is unknown, it's safe to say they were either a genius or incredibly fortunate, as this is most definitely a 'majestic' philodendron. Exhibiting traits of both parent plants, *Philodendron sodiroi* and *Philodendron verrucosum*, it is a beautiful rarity that will live its best life in a greenhouse with access to consistently high humidity.

Philodendron melanochrysum

Philodendron squamiferum

COMMON NAME RED BRISTLE PHILODENDRON

The *Philodendron squamiferum*'s standout feature is its bristly red-tinged stems from which the plant also gets its common name.

CARE LEVEL
novice

LIGHT
bright, indirect

WATER
moderate

SOIL
well-draining

HUMIDITY
medium

PROPAGATION
stem cuttings

GROWTH HABIT
climbing

POSITION
tabletop + floor

TOXICITY
toxic

These stems first emerge chartreuse-pink before turning red with their signature hairy texture. The foliage features five distinctive lobes that become more pronounced as the plant matures. This adaptable philodendron, endemic to Colombia, Peru and Brazil can handle a range of conditions (as long as it's warm), thus making it a happy houseplant indeed.

Position in bright, indirect light, avoiding harsh sun that will burn its glossy leaves. It has moderate water needs so allow the top 5 cm (2 in) of soil to dry out between drinks. This rainforest dweller will appreciate weekly misting, and be sure to keep those large, luscious leaves dust free with a regular wipe down using a clean cloth or a soft-hair brush.

Philodendron tatei ssp. melanochlorum 'Congo'

COMMON NAME CONGO PHILODENDRON

This philodendron cultivar has a self-heading growth habit that, much like the *Philodendron erubescens* on page 95, grows outwards and upwards, peaking at about 60 cm (2 ft) in both height and width.

CARE LEVEL
novice

LIGHT
bright, indirect

WATER
moderate

SOIL
well-draining

HUMIDITY
medium

PROPAGATION
stem cuttings

GROWTH HABIT
clumping

POSITION
floor + covered balcony

TOXICITY
toxic

Sold in a range of colours, this is one of several cultivars of philodendron that has been recently developed by growers.

The 'rojo Congo' (pictured here) displays striking large leaves that emerge coppery-red, maturing to deep burgundy and then finally to dark green, with stems and petioles (leaf stalks) that retain a rich red hue. The regular Congo, on the other hand, sports all-green foliage but with the same smooth-edged, oval-shaped leaves.

Caring for these hardy and tolerant philodendrons is easy-as. Apart from extreme cold they will withstand a variety of conditions and, as such, work well both indoors or on covered balconies. Bright, indirect light (lots of it for the 'rojo Congo') is best. The Congo will handle short periods of drought, but ideally water once the top 5 cm (2 in) of soil is dry. Keep in mind that if exposed to lots of bright light, you will need to water your Congo more regularly.

Philodendron tortum

SKELETON KEY PHILODENDRON

Endemic to Colombia and Brazil, the *Philodendron tortum* is no ordinary houseplant. Sporting spindly, multi-stemmed foliage, it is referred to commonly as the skeleton key philodendron.

CARE LEVEL
novice

LIGHT
bright, indirect

WATER
high

SOIL
well-draining

HUMIDITY
high

PROPAGATION
stem cuttings

GROWTH HABIT
climbing

POSITION
tabletop

TOXICITY
toxic

New leaves unfurl in a corkscrew to reveal this plant's unusual and unique aesthetic. Enjoy the texturual interest this sculptural beauty will bring to your indoor jungle, as this sought-after houseplant definitely stands out from the crowd.

In the wild, this epiphytic vine starts its life in the ground as a tiny seedling looking to make its way up in the world, climbing towards the rainforest canopy as it matures. At home you can stake the plant for support or embrace its natural stature and let it grow freely. Despite its rarity, the skeleton key philodendron grows happily indoors with minimal fuss. While the true species plants are exceptionally cold-sensitive, those grown from tissue-culture are sufficiently hardier, and while they may lose a few leaves come winter, the plant won't typically go dormant.

Like most philodendrons, it enjoys a spot with plenty of bright, indirect light. Pot in a well-draining, aerated soil mix and water deeply once the top 5 cm (2 in) of potting mix has dried out, always making sure to empty the saucer 30 minutes after watering. The delicate nature of the jagged foliage means you do need to be careful when tending to *P. tortum* to avoid unfortunate mishaps.

Aeschynanthus

Comprising 150 species of subtropical and tropical plants that are typically trailing epiphytes with brightly coloured flowers, the genus name *Aeschynanthus* is derived from a combination of the Latin *aischuno* (to be ashamed) and *anthos* (flower). 'Shame-flower' is the collective name for the genus in the same way that elephant ears describe *Alocasia* and flamingo flowers describe *Anthurium*.

The plants within this genus are incredibly varied. Some sport thick, waxy cuticles, while others have much softer leaves; however, the species most commonly kept as houseplants, including *A. longicaulis* and *A. radicans* (see opposite), are similar in appearance and referred to as lipstick plants for their developing buds that resemble a tube of lipstick. While differentiated by the colouration of their foliage and blooms, their care requirements are pretty much the same. These tropical beauties like it nice and steamy, with a brief period of cooler temperatures in winter to stimulate the flowers for which they are commonly known.

CARE LEVEL
novice

LIGHT
bright, indirect

WATER
moderate

SOIL
well-draining

HUMIDITY
medium

PROPAGATION
stem cuttings

GROWTH HABIT
trailing

POSITION
bookshelf or stand

TOXICITY
pet friendly

Aeschynanthus radicans

COMMON NAME **LIPSTICK PLANT**

The waxy green ovate leaves of the lipstick plant cascade beautifully, growing up to 1.5 metres (5 ft) in the wild. Although slightly more contained indoors – 90 cm (3 ft) in optimum conditions – add some clusters of their signature red and burgundy blooms into the mix and you have yourself one striking indoor plant.

The *Aeschynanthus radicans* will thrive indoors with the right care. Native to the humid tropics of Malaysia and Indonesia, it requires good levels of humidity, which can be achieved through regular misting. Although it grows epiphytically on other trees in its natural environment, indoors it responds well to an aerated and well-draining potting mix. It is possible to grow lipstick plants mounted to a wooden board or a cork bark slab (as you would an orchid), but it's important to note that you will need to water it more frequently to ensure that it stays adequately hydrated.

For a bushy, full lipstick plant and to encourage blooms, prune back the long stems (about one-third of their length) with a sharp pair of secateurs after blooming has finished. This will prevent the growth becoming leggy and looking straggly.

specimen *Ficus elastica* ˈtinekeˈ

Ficus

This genus, consisting of more than 850 species, is named after the edible fig. Predominantly evergreen and hailing mainly from the tropics of Africa and Asia, it is the species that germinate in the semi-darkness of the forest floor that are the best suited to the conditions of our homes. From the glossy and robust rubber plant (*Ficus elastica*; see page 127) to the sacred and seductive Bengal fig (*Ficus benghalensis*; see page 120) these rainforest dwellers have become some of the most popular houseplants around. No wonder, as the extraordinary foliage and air-purifying skills of these beauties are too good to resist.

Ficus benghalensis 'Audrey'

COMMON NAME BENGAL FIG

Revered in its native home of India, the Bengal fig (or banyan fig, as it is also known) is believed to be the tree under which the Buddha sat to achieve enlightenment.

CARE LEVEL
novice

LIGHT
bright, indirect

WATER
moderate

SOIL
well-draining

HUMIDITY
medium

PROPAGATION
stem cuttings

GROWTH HABIT
upright

POSITION
floor

TOXICITY
toxic

These leafy giants are some of the largest trees in the world by area of canopy coverage, and they provide great shade for other plants in their native environment.

Indoors, the *Ficus benghalensis* works beautifully as a statement plant in a large living area or workspace. This delightful ornamental tree is a great air-purifier and offers a unique alternative to some of the better known figs. Its glorious rich, green oval-shaped leaves are intersected with pale green veins, creating a striking juxtaposition. With a thick trunk and bushy top, we love its tree-like stature.

The Bengal fig is generally more tolerant of inconsistent watering schedules and changes in temperature and humidity than its cousin *Ficus lyrata*. It thrives in bright, indirect light and will even tolerate a small amount of direct sunlight or low-light conditions. Easy-going seems an understatement! *F. benghalensis* will benefit from fertiliser diluted to half strength in the summer months, but lay off in the cooler seasons when its growth slows. It's worth noting that its sap is quite toxic so be careful when pruning, and keep away from kids and pets.

Ficus benjamina

COMMON NAME WEEPING FIG

Sporting dainty leaves that dangle from its fine branches, *Ficus benjamina* gets its common name from its weeping growth habit. Ironically, it also accurately describes its tendency to shed leaves at the drop of a hat, for this can be a fussy ficus indeed.

CARE LEVEL
green thumb

LIGHT
bright, indirect

WATER
moderate

SOIL
well-draining

HUMIDITY
medium–high

PROPAGATION
stem cuttings

GROWTH HABIT
upright

POSITION
floor

TOXICITY
toxic

There are a number of scenarios that can put this sensitive fig under stress and trigger those leaves to fall. While this effective communicator is not shy in coming forward to let you know it's unhappy, it can be quite the process of elimination to determine exactly what is going wrong. From under- or over-watering or dissatisfaction at being relocated, through to possible pest infestation or exposure to a draught, the weeping fig can be pretty unforgiving.

That said, with access to bright, indirect light and a consistent watering schedule that allows only the top 2–5 cm (¾–2 in) of soil to dry out between drinks, this attractive indoor tree can thrive, rewarding attentive plant parents. In favourable conditions, *F. benjamina* is a fairly rapid grower and an effective air-purifier. You will do well to maintain relatively high levels of humidity around the plant through regular misting. To promote growth, fertilise once a month in spring and summer.

Ficus binnendijkii

COMMON NAME SABRE FIG

This tall and dainty fig, with thin and pointy dark-olive leaves reminiscent of an Australian native, is elegantly proportioned.

CARE LEVEL
novice

LIGHT
bright, indirect

WATER
medium

SOIL
well-draining

HUMIDITY
medium

PROPAGATION
stem cuttings

GROWTH HABIT
upright

POSITION
floor +
covered balcony

TOXICITY
toxic

Ficus binnendijkii is an ideal container plant for both indoors and out – a covered balcony provides the perfect home.

Sabre figs are fairly slow growers, but they look beautiful at any size. They produce a dense mass of foliage, but as the plant matures it may drop its lower leaves revealing a woody trunk. To encourage growth, we recommend repotting every two years at the end of winter, but be sure to increase your planter size gradually as they prefer to be slightly pot bound. Sabre figs enjoy bright, indirect light, but will tolerate lower-light conditions as well.

A relatively new cultivar of the sabre fig, the Ficus 'alii petite' (pictured here) doesn't exist in the wild but it makes a fantastic houseplant. You'll find the dwarf cultivar less temperamental as it doesn't tend to drop leaves (unless seriously over- or under-watered), plus it's relatively pest and disease resistant. Its toxic sap does, however, mean that it's not safe for pets. To keep your sabre fig looking its best, feed with a half-strength liquid fertiliser once a month in spring and summer.

Ficus elastica 'robusta'

Ficus elastica

COMMON NAME RUBBER PLANT

With robust, lustrous leaves and the capacity to grow nice and large, the *Ficus elastica* is one strapping specimen of fig. With an upright growth habit that makes it well suited to a position on the floor, mature specimens in particular make a strong statement in a bright corner or on a covered balcony.

CARE LEVEL
novice

LIGHT
bright, indirect

WATER
moderate

SOIL
well-draining

HUMIDITY
medium

PROPAGATION
stem cuttings

GROWTH HABIT
upright

POSITION
floor

TOXICITY
toxic

This hardy fig is low maintenance and will even let a little neglect slide. It will communicate its thirst by wilting, and its leaves may also curl after long periods of drought. Avoid getting to this point by implementing a regular watering schedule. A good soak roughly once a week should do the trick, but as long as the top 5 cm (2 in) of soil has dried out, you are good to water again. The rubber plant's wide leaves gather dust easily, so wipe them down regularly with a damp cloth. A regular spray of white or eco-oil will keep the leaves looking super glossy with the added benefit of keeping pests at bay. Avoid hot and cold draughts, as the rubber plant can be sensitive to drastic changes in temperature. As with all figs, the sap can cause irritation on contact as well as if ingested, so keep clear of pesky pets and curious little ones.

With a range of variegated options also available – from mottled cream, green and blush-coloured 'tineke', to the moodier red tones of the 'ruby' – *Ficus elastica* can add colour and pizzazz to your indoor jungle. Keep in mind that to maintain the stunning patterning on variegated foliage, these guys have higher light requirements than their non-variegated cousins.

Ficus elastica 'tineke'

Ficus elastica 'burgundy'

Ficus lyrata

COMMON NAME **FIDDLE-LEAF FIG**

The voluptuous fiddle-shaped leaves of the *Ficus lyrata* continue to grace the pages of interiors magazines, with the popularity of this deliciously retro plant showing no sign of waning.

CARE LEVEL
green thumb

LIGHT
bright, indirect

WATER
moderate

SOIL
well-draining

HUMIDITY
medium–high

PROPAGATION
stem cuttings

GROWTH HABIT
upright

POSITION
floor

TOXICITY
toxic

Whether multi-stemmed and bushy, or bare stemmed with a burst of growth at the top of the plant, the fiddle-leaf fig adds an architectural elegance to any interior.

Having fallen madly in love with this fig's good looks, many unsuspecting plant parents have excitedly secured one only to discover within weeks of bringing her home that she can be a fickle mistress. She'll certainly make you work for those good looks. The *F. lyrata* is a demanding diva, but quite frankly she's worth the effort!

Fiddle-leaf figs have relatively high light requirements – indirect is best as direct sun will blemish those precious leaves. A deep soaking once a week or so is generally adequate, but ensure the top 5 cm (2 in) of soil is completely dry before watering again. The *F. lyrata* appreciates high humidity – dry air from heaters and air conditioners is particularly damaging and can leave the plant susceptible to infestations of sucking pests, such as spider mites.

Keep large foliage dust free by giving the leaves a regular clean. Spraying with eco-oil as part of your maintenance regime will help keep pests at bay and has the added benefit of adding glorious shine to the fiddle's foliage. Rotate the plant routinely to maintain even growth as these beauties tend to grow towards a light source and can end up a little lop-sided.

Ultimately, once settled in a bright position and with consistency of care, the fiddle-leaf fig will delight as it reaches for the ceiling. Just make sure you have room to accommodate this lush indoor tree.

Ficus petiolaris

COMMON NAME ROCK FIG

A swollen stem base (caudex) and fabulous foliage dissected by pretty pink veins makes the *Ficus petiolaris* one of the more unique figs.

CARE LEVEL
novice

LIGHT
bright, indirect

WATER
moderate

SOIL
well-draining

HUMIDITY
medium

PROPAGATION
stem cuttings

GROWTH HABIT
upright

POSITION
floor

TOXICITY
toxic

Endemic to Mexico, the rock fig grows (unsurprisingly) in rocky areas where the roots stretch over rocks in search of soil.

Known as a caudiciform or 'fat plant', the swollen root or stem of the rock fig is used to store food and water, which affords the plant periods of survival in drought-prone and nutrient-poor environments. For this reason, it is best to let the top 5 cm (2 in) of soil dry out before watering again, as it is more adept at handling drier conditions than most. Rock figs develop their large and distinctive woody caudex at an early age making them a popular bonsai tree.

This characterful fig makes an excellent houseplant with a low-maintenance M.O. Potted in well-draining soil and kept in a spot with bright, indirect light, the *Ficus petiolaris* will thrive. While adorable at any size, if you want this fig to grow large give it a home with some room to move and fertilise regularly in the warmer months.

Fittonia

Fittonia are native to South American tropical rainforests where they grow by spreading along the ground. These petite plants, both in leaf size and stature, reach heights of only about 15 cm (6 in), making them perfect specimens for people living in smaller spaces.

Their fabulous little yellow, green or red leaves, filled with colourful white, red or pink veins, make for a rainbow-like collection of plants. *Fittonia gigantea*, the largest leaf member of this small, three-member genus, usually has more subtly coloured leaves, while the leaves of the *Fittonia verschaffeltii* are probably the loudest.

CARE LEVEL
novice

LIGHT
low–moderate

WATER
moderate

SOIL
well-draining

HUMIDITY
medium

PROPAGATION
stem cuttings

GROWTH HABIT
clumping

POSITION
tabletop

TOXICITY
pet friendly

Fittonia albivenis

COMMON NAME NERVE PLANT

One of only three species in the *Fittonia* genus, the dramatic leaves of the nerve plant pack quite a punch despite their small size. With usually white, but sometimes pink or even red veins, contrasting against the green leaves, they add colour and pattern to any plant collection. This plant meanders along the rainforest floor in its native Bolivia, Brazil, Colombia, Ecuador and Peru, while in pots it will stay compact with a bit of pruning, or slowly creep over the edge if allowed to do so.

Similar to peace lilies, *Fittonia albivenis* will loudly communicate its thirst by dramatically drooping its leaves. But rather than making it yell for attention, try and keep your plant happy by watering it once the top 2 cm (¾ in) of soil has dried out. Never let the pot sit in a saucer filled with excess water. Although it will thrive in bright, indirect light, nerve plants are also highly tolerant of lower-light conditions and will even survive under fluorescent lighting. Given that it's not a heavy feeder, a monthly top-up with half-strength liquid fertiliser should do the trick.

Thanks to its petite size and penchant for humidity, nerve plants work beautifully in terrariums. As the decorative foliage, rather than the fairly insignificant flowers, is the main attraction here, many growers snip off the flowers as they appear so the plant doesn't 'waste' energy on them. All in all these guys are pretty low maintenance and make a graphic addition to an indoor jungle.

Strelitzia

A very well known but relatively small genus of only five species, *Strelitzia* are commonly named after birds of paradise or crowned crane birds for which their often brightly coloured flowers resemble. Native to South Africa, these subtropical plants have found their way onto the back of the South African 50 cent coin, and have also become the floral emblem of Los Angeles.

The genus's Latin name is an ode to Queen Charlotte, King George III's wife, who was born in the northern German duchy of Mecklenburg-Strelitz. As an amateur botanist, she helped expand the famous Kew Gardens of London and was thus rewarded with this taxonomic honour.

Strelitzia are pollinated by birds rather than insects, and in a beautiful example of the intelligence of nature and evolution, the flower is designed to open under the weight of a bird resting on its elongated modified petals. The plant then gently dusts the bird's feathers with pollen, which the bird then carries and helps to pollinate the next flower.

Strelitzia nicolai

COMMON NAME GIANT WHITE BIRD OF PARADISE

Strelitzia nicolai is by far the tallest of its genus, reaching heights of 10 metres (33 ft) under optimum outdoor conditions. Indoors, they will still get big, but most likely stay under a couple of metres (roughly 6 ft).

CARE LEVEL
novice

LIGHT
bright, indirect

WATER
moderate–high

SOIL
well-draining

HUMIDITY
low

PROPAGATION
division + offsets

GROWTH HABIT
clumping

POSITION
floor + covered balcony

TOXICITY
mildly toxic

The giant white bird of paradise has large grey-green leathery leaves, with spectacular blue and white flowers that appear from a dusty charcoal spathe once the plant matures. Unfortunately, indoors it is unlikely to bloom unless it's receiving a tonne of direct sunlight throughout the day. It uses a lot of energy to produce its giant leaves, so use a rich soil and top it up with a fortnightly dose of liquid fertiliser during the growing season. As an added boost, you can top dress the pot with the appropriate potting mix with added slow-release fertiliser. It's worth noting that top dressing is only necessary if you're in a 'year off' of potting up, but lacking enough quality top soil.

Strelitzia enjoy a warm environment and low to moderate humidity, so the average indoor climate is perfect. Water deeply, soaking the potting mix so it drains out the base of the pot. In spring and summer, allow the top 2–5 cm (¾–2 in) of soil to dry out before watering again, but back off a bit in winter. If you're strong enough to lift the heavier pots, these plants will benefit from being placed outdoors during a rainstorm, as they prefer distilled water to tap.

Clean the large leaves with a damp cloth or in the shower, and keep in mind that they are prone to ripping so be as gentle as possible, but if they do, don't fret, as this is a natural occurrence that doesn't impact the plant's health. Applying an eco-oil will keep the leaves glossy and help avert any curious pests, but be sure to wipe it off fully before exposing the foliage to any direct sunlight.

Strelitzia reginae

COMMON NAME BIRD OF PARADISE

This delightfully easy-care plant has large, upright, grey-green paddle-shaped leaves, from which protrude the orange, red and regal blue flowers that lend this plant its common name.

CARE LEVEL
novice

LIGHT
bright, indirect

WATER
moderate

SOIL
well-draining

HUMIDITY
low

PROPAGATION
division

GROWTH HABIT
clumping

POSITION
floor + covered balcony

TOXICITY
mildly toxic

Strelitzia reginae, was first introduced into the UK in 1773, and was formally described by botanist Sir Joseph Banks at the Royal Botanic Gardens in Kew in 1788. Since then, it has become a hugely popular plant both indoors and out, lining many a street in California and greening indoor spaces all over the world.

These plants will tolerate a little neglect (they're semi-drought tolerant), but try to stick to a regular watering schedule, giving your plant a big drink once the top 5 cm (2 in) of soil has dried out in summer, dropping back in winter. Birds of paradise absolutely do not tolerate sitting in a puddle of their own water, so be sure to empty saucers post watering. Fertilise with a half-strength liquid fertiliser every three weeks in the warmer months.

Although less likely to flower indoors, with enough direct sun you might just be in luck. But do not despair if you don't, as the leaves alone, especially once the plant reaches maturity, are a great hero in any living room or covered balcony. Either way, make sure this plant does receive some direct sunlight – gentle morning rays are best.

To keep your plant tidy, remove spent flowers and leaves and wipe down the leaves with a damp cloth. While birds of paradise are not necessarily the fastest growers above the soil, their roots grow thick, fast and strong and have a tendency to bust through their pots (Incredible Hulk, eat your heart out), so it's a good idea to repot them at the start of spring so they have room to expand during the growing season. To avoid ceramic pot fatalities, we recommend planting your *Strelitzia reginae* in a plastic grow pot inside a larger cachepot.

Begonia

Named after the 17th century French naturalist and passionate plant collector Michel Bégon, *Begonia* are a fantastically diverse collection of plants appreciated for their sweet flowers and fabulous foliage. The leaves encompass a varied spectrum of shapes, textures, edging and colours, with some forming spirals that resemble snail shells, while others have distinct, painted markings, or are velvety to the touch. Their blooms are equally diverse, from single pendulous blossoms, to clusters of antique rose-like flowers.

Categorising begonias can be a little tricky and convoluted, but they can generally be divided into the following groups: rhizomatous, cane-stem, tuberous, wax and rex begonias. Wax begonias are hybrids originating from *Begonia cucullata*. Rex begonias are a subgroup of rhizomatous begonias, which are hybrids descending from the Indian species *Begonia rex*. Semantics aside, begonias are pretty as a picture and generally easy to care for, so it's time to get acquainted with this prolific genus that make fabulous houseplants.

specimen *Begonia maculata*

Begonia bowerae

EYELASH BEGONIA

Referred to commonly as the eyelash begonia for the erect white hairs that line the leaves' edges, *Begonia bowerae* is a rhizomatous begonia with some seriously spectacular foliage. The leaves are deep emerald green with dark markings along the edges and sometimes along the leaf veins, too.

CARE LEVEL
green thumb

LIGHT
bright, indirect

WATER
moderate

SOIL
well-draining

HUMIDITY
high

PROPAGATION
leaf cuttings + division

GROWTH HABIT
clumping

POSITION
tabletop

TOXICITY
toxic

If those lovely leaves aren't enough, with plenty of bright, indirect light, come early spring it produces loose clusters of pretty white or light pink shell-shaped flowers held on thin pink stems above the foliage.

Begonia bowerae is a miniature begonia native to Mexico, where it grows as ground cover on the tropical forest floor and only reaches heights of about 25 cm (10 in). Keep humidity high for this moisture lover by grouping it with other plants or sitting on a pebble-filled saucer of water. Misting and generally getting the leaves wet is to be avoided, as it can encourage the growth of powdery mildew.

Being a rhizomatous begonia with shallow roots, it is best to plant the eyelash begonia in a shallow pot with a well-draining potting mix. A brightly lit position with good ventilation will also be appreciated. Pinching the tips and pruning the outer stems in the warmer seasons will promote bushier growth that works well displayed atop a table.

Begonia bowerae cultivars and hybrids, with their ornately patterned leaves, as well as a propensity for rapid growth, have seen them rise to prominence in the indoor plant world. One such cultivar, *Begonia bowerae* × 'tiger paws' (pictured), a hybrid developed in 1977, sports small brownish leaves that are chequered with yellow markings said to resemble, funnily enough, a tiger's paw.

Begonia brevirimosa

COMMON NAME EXOTIC BEGONIA

Some plants were born to stand out, and with its large metallic leaves of dark green topped with luminous pink variegation, the *Begonia brevirimosa* demands attention.

CARE LEVEL
green thumb

LIGHT
bright, indirect

WATER
moderate–high

SOIL
well-draining

HUMIDITY
high

PROPAGATION
leaf cuttings + division

GROWTH HABIT
clumping

POSITION
tabletop

TOXICITY
toxic

Those leaves will become more pink in brightly lit, warm and humid environments, while cooler, darker conditions can see the variegation fade. Its pretty pink flowers can appear year round, but don't be discouraged if it doesn't flower indoors as there's enough to admire without them.

Abundant in the understory of the tropical rainforests of New Guinea, it may be surprising to know that the exotic begonia is a naturally occurring species rather than a cultivated hybrid. Described as having a shrub-like, clumping growth habit, this begonia makes a wonderful houseplant as long as its basic needs are met.

To meet its humidity needs you can group it with other humidity-loving plants or if you're really serious, a humidifier will do the trick. For this reason it will also do well in terreriums and greenhouses.

Keep the potting mix consistently moist, allowing only the very top layer to dry out between watering. Its stems and foliage will droop considerably if dehydrated but avoid getting to that point. It may be a little more work than some plants, but we think it's a small price to pay for this absolute showstopper.

Begonia maculata

COMMON NAME POLKA DOT BEGONIA

While there is no shortage of photogenic houseplants, particularly in the *Begonia* genus, the *Begonia maculata* or polka dot begonia has got to be up there as one of the prettiest.

CARE LEVEL
novice

LIGHT
bright, indirect

WATER
moderate

SOIL
well-draining

HUMIDITY
medium

PROPAGATION
leaf cuttings + division

GROWTH HABIT
upright

POSITION
tabletop

TOXICITY
toxic

Large, angel wing–shaped leaves, patterned with silver spots on top and a deep purple-red on the undersides, ensure that this plant is a real eyecatcher.

Classified as a cane begonia, *Begonia maculata*'s thick, cane-like stems promote fairly upright growth, but the way the wing-shaped leaves suspend also means it works equally well in a hanging planter or tabletop vessel. One of the most popular classes of begonia for their hardiness (and beauty), it is especially suitable for houseplant culture. This decidedly unfussy plant has moderate light and water requirements, and can be happily looked after by gardeners of all levels. Bright, indirect light is ideal and while it will tolerate lower light, it's worth noting that such conditions will alter the plant's signature colourations and variegation, particularly in the case of *Begonia maculata* 'wightii' (pictured here), which will lose its red undersides and relax its leaf shape to its detriment. Too much direct afternoon sun can cause leaves to dry or burn, so keep it protected from harsh light conditions.

Try to keep the soil fairly moist in spring and summer, only allowing the top 2–5 cm (¾–2 in) to dry out between drinks. Although the *Begonia maculata* doesn't go dormant in winter, its growth slows and its water needs are lower, so be sure to hold back as the weather cools.

Begonia mazae

MAZAE BEGONIA

Don't let its size fool you, the *Begonia mazae* may be a compact specimen, but it will have a serious impact in your indoor jungle.

CARE LEVEL
green thumb

LIGHT
bright, indirect

WATER
moderate

SOIL
well-draining

HUMIDITY
medium–high

PROPAGATION
leaf cuttings + division

GROWTH HABIT
trailing

POSITION
bookshelf or stand

TOXICITY
toxic

Tear-shaped, dark green leaves overlaid with a blackish pattern make for a bold and moody plant. In the right conditions, the leaves glow with a velvety sheen that gives further lushness and depth to this tactile beauty.

It is classified as a scandent variety due to its heavy foliage, which weighs down its slender stems causing the plant to trail downwards. As such, the *B. mazae* is suited to an elevated position, such as a bookshelf or even a hanging planter.

It also responds well to pinching, making it easy to achieve a full, bushy begonia. For added delight, in spring and summer large sprays of small pink flowers appear on slender stems above the dark foliage, making a beautiful spectacle.

Begonia mazea will do best in a consistently moist, well-draining potting mix. Keep humidity moderately high, but avoid applying moisture directly to the foliage. A bright position, sheltered from direct sun with good air circulation, is ideal.

Begonia peltata

COMMON NAME **FUZZY LEAF BEGONIA**

Sporting distinctive silver-grey, felt-like leaves, this textural plant is commonly referred to as the fuzzy leaf begonia.

CARE LEVEL
green thumb

LIGHT
bright, indirect

WATER
moderate–high

SOIL
well-draining

HUMIDITY
medium

PROPAGATION
leaf cuttings + division

GROWTH HABIT
clumping

POSITION
tabletop

TOXICITY
toxic

Begonia peltata's almost round foliage is covered in short, soft hairs that, as with other hairy-leaved plants, are actually specialised epidermal cells that help protect against insects and moisture loss. Extending above its tactile foliage, the produces sprays of white blooms that usually appear from late winter into spring.

Treat it right and the fuzzy leaf begonia will thrive indoors. Warm, humid conditions work best for this plant and good air circulation will help keep pests and disease that thrive in damp conditions at bay. A well-draining potting mix should be allowed to just dry out between drinks; however, it will tolerate a bit of dryness better than many begonias. A feed with half-strength liquid fertiliser once or twice a month will promote rapid healthy growth, resulting in an attractive, bushy begonia in no time. Just try keeping your hands off this bad boy!

Begonia rex

PAINTED LEAF BEGONIA

Commonly referred to as fancy leaf or painted begonias and described by the American Begonia Society as 'the showboat of the begonia world', these guys are grown almost exclusively for their fabulous foliage.

CARE LEVEL
green thumb

LIGHT
bright, indirect

WATER
moderate

SOIL
moisture-retaining

HUMIDITY
high

PROPAGATION
leaf cuttings + division

GROWTH HABIT
clumping

POSITION
tabletop

TOXICITY
toxic

'Rex' means 'king' in Latin, which is a fitting name for this species with the biggest, most extravagant leaves. Shaped like lopsided hearts, they come naturally decorated in an array of pinks, purples, greens, browns, reds and even silver. While the flowers are somewhat insignificant, it doesn't matter when the foliage looks this good!

All rex begonias, of which there are hundreds of cultivars and hybrids to choose from, include the wild species *Begonia rex* in their parentage. While they can live happily indoors, they have a firm objection to the dry air of our homes that can lead to browning leaf edges and eventually leaf drop. It is for this reason that they are considered tricky to care for by some, but with the right attention they will thrive.

These rhizomatous stunners like it moist and will do best in rich, aerated, but still moisture-retaining soil that is similar to that found on the forest floor of their native home in northeastern India, southern China, Vietnam and the Galápagos Islands. High humidity is essential, but avoid misting the leaves as it can lead to the formation of powdery mildew. Instead, group the *Begonia rex* with other humidity-loving plants or sit it on a saucer of pebbles and water. It's worth noting that many cultivars experience dormancy in winter as the leaves naturally begin to yellow and fall. Although decidedly less attractive in this state, it will make a glorious return once warmer, brighter conditions signal that it's safe to push out fresh growth.

Caladium

Another member of the Araceae family, *Caladium* is a genus of flowering plants commonly referred to as heart of Jesus, angel wings or elephant ear (a name shared with the closely related *Alocasia*, *Colocasia* and *Xanthosoma* genera). Their beautifully patterned and colourful heart- or arrow-shaped leaves have resulted in several species being grown as ornamental plants that survive well indoors, the most widely cultivated being the 'fancy-leaved' and 'lance-leaved' forms.

These colourful beauties, with foliage marked white, pink or red, are native to South and Central America, as well as being naturalised in India and parts of Africa. In the wild, they grow between 60 and 90 cm (2–3 ft) in height, with leaves reaching up to 45 cm (18 in) in length, although cultivated varieties are generally slightly more petite. Caladiums grow from tubers and can be easily propagated by means of division.

Caladium bicolor

COMMON NAME FANCY LEAF CALADIUM

This colourful caladium hails from the tropical forests of South America, where it produces seasonal foliage during the warm rainy season.

CARE LEVEL
green thumb

LIGHT
bright, indirect

WATER
high

SOIL
well-draining

HUMIDITY
high

PROPAGATION
division

GROWTH HABIT
clumping

POSITION
tabletop

TOXICITY
toxic

All caladiums are perennial tubers that become dormant in winter, springing back to life in the growing season, so be sure to enjoy them for their colour and pizzazz through the warmer months, and let them get their beauty rest once the weather cools. As their leaves start to fade and drop during this time, simply remove them by cutting with a sharp pair of secateurs at the base of their stem.

Providing high levels of humidity is crucial to the survival of fancy leaf caladiums in our all too often dry homes. Regular misting – daily if possible – will be much appreciated. Additionally, try placing your plant on a saucer filled with pebbles and water, as the evaporation moistens the ambient air and helps provide the necessary humidity. Keep the well-draining potting mix consistently moist during the growing period, allowing only the top layer of soil to dry out; however you will need to scale right back once the plant loses its foliage.

There are more than 1000 cultivars of *Caladium bicolor*. Pictured here is the *C. bicolor* 'red belly' that features bright green leaves with a splash of red in the centre.

Caladium lindenii

COMMON NAME WHITE VEIN ARROW LEAF

A true showstopper in every sense of the word, the fabulous foliage on this Colombian native is gloriously graphic. Its large leaves, thin and leathery in texture and shaped like arrowheads, are yellow-green with striking, broad white veins.

CARE LEVEL
green thumb

LIGHT
bright, indirect

WATER
high

SOIL
well-draining

HUMIDITY
high

PROPAGATION
division

GROWTH HABIT
clumping

POSITION
tabletop

TOXICITY
toxic

You will sometimes find the *Caladium lindenii* labelled as *Xanthosoma lindenii*, even though it was reclassified in the early 1980s. It seems old habits die hard.

Warmth, bright but indirect light and plenty of humidity will encourage healthy growth that will see this herbaceous shrub form a dense clump reaching 60–90 cm (2–3 ft) in height. A monthly feed with a half-strength liquid fertiliser will further optimise growth, and regular misting of the foliage is advised. Rich, moist, but well-draining potting mix is your best bet, which can be achieved by adding some coco coir to your regular potting mix.

Caladium lindenii has a tendency towards the dramatic, particularly when it comes to over-watering, but it can also collapse when dehydrated, so getting the balance right is key. In cooler climates, it will often take the winter off growing, and in seriously cold climates it may go completely dormant. In these instances, you should stop watering almost completely until you see signs of growth as the weather warms up.

Thanks to their tuberous roots, the *Caladium lindenii* is incredibly easy to propagate by means of division. Just be careful handling the plant as it can cause skin irritation for some people. You'll also need to keep it away from curious pets and small humans.

Aglaonema

Aglaonema, or Chinese evergreen, is a genus of flowering plants in the Araceae family that have been grown as luck-bringing ornamental plants in Asia for centuries. Consisting of only around 25 species, they have been cultivated and hybridised into hundreds of varieties, exhibiting an incredibly diverse range of foliage colourations and patterns. It's very common to find Chinese evergreen plants referred to by their cultivar names rather than their true botanical names, which can make identification difficult. It's worth battling through the confusion though, as their mottled foliage in combinations of red, pink, silver, green and cream add striking beauty to any indoor garden.

Native to tropical and subtropical areas of Asia, Chinese evergreens are popular as houseplants, not only for their beauty but for their ease of care, air-purifying qualities and an ability to tolerate lower-light conditions. Some of the darker green varieties can even survive in spaces with only artificial light.

CARE LEVEL
novice

LIGHT
low–moderate

WATER
moderate

SOIL
well-draining

HUMIDITY
medium

PROPAGATION
stem cuttings

GROWTH HABIT
clumping

POSITION
tabletop

TOXICITY
toxic

Aglaonema 'stripes'

COMMON NAME CHINESE EVERGREEN

Beautiful and easy to care for, the *Aglaonema* 'stripes' is a double treat, with rich green leaves patterned with narrow bands of silvery-white stripes. As with all aglaonemas, it will survive in low light, but you may notice the plant becoming thin and leggy. Bright, indirect light will encourage the healthiest growth, but even consistent artificial fluorescent light will do, making it a popular choice for large office spaces where natural light is hard to come by.

Aglaonema 'stripes' looks best when it's full and bushy, which can be achieved by taking a few small stem cuttings from the tip of the plant (ideally in spring when the plant is in active growth), and then rooting in water before replanting back into the pot they came from. The cane-like stems will then likely reshoot more than one dormant bud.

This tropical beauty prefers a warm temperate environment, but as long as it is kept dry and in a protected spot, it can withstand cooler temperatures. You can also prolong its life by removing inflorescences as they develop to allow the plant to focus its energy on producing healthy leaf growth rather than insignificant blooms. To remove the flowers, wait until their stalks become yellow and soft, then simply pluck them off.

specimen *Anthurium veitchii*

Anthurium

Anthurium is the largest genus within the broader Araceae family, containing around 1000 species of flowering plants. Native to the neotropics of South America, Mexico and the Caribbean, they are quite partial to the conditions of life indoors or temperate, protected outdoor spots, where they often grow epiphytically on trees. A defining feature of this species is the flower-like spathe (which is actually a modified leaf), from which grows an often phallic-shaped spadix that produces tiny bisexual flowers.

Anthurium has some of the greatest species diversity of any genus, and it is also known to be highly variable, meaning that even if you have two plants of the same species they might not look totally alike. From the brilliant turtle shell–like patterns of the crystal anthurium (*Anthurium crystallinum*) to the dramatic slender leaves of the strap-leaf anthurium (*Anthurium vittarifolium*) and everything in between, these plants are brilliantly unique and visually spectacular.

Anthurium polydactylum

COMMON NAME POLYDACTYLUM ANTHURIUM

The combination of grey-green colouring and palmate form make this a rather special houseplant. Collected by *Anthurium* lovers around the world, it requires a little more care than some stock-standard houseplants, but we assure you it's worth the effort.

CARE LEVEL
green thumb

LIGHT
bright, indirect

WATER
moderate

SOIL
well-draining

HUMIDITY
high

PROPAGATION
division

GROWTH HABIT
climbing

POSITION
tabletop

TOXICITY
toxic

Similar in name and looks to the *Anthurium polyschistum* (faux marijuana plant), it's easy to get these plants confused. The *A. polydactylum*, has slim finger-like leaflets with smooth edges, and it is notably larger in both leaf size and stem length that its sister plant. It's also sometimes compared to the more readily available *Schefflera*, which makes a good alternative if you can't get your hands on this rare beauty. This anthurium is native to Bolivia, Colombia and Peru, and finds itself everywhere from low-altitude swamps where it grows along the ground, to the high altitudes of the Andes mountains where it climbs into the trees the higher up it is found.

Polydactylum anthurium likes bright, indirect light and moist but never soggy soil. It will also greatly benefit from high humidity, so get spritzing. Once it has moved on from its smaller juvenile stage it will need to be staked to manage growth.

Anthurium balaoanum
Hailing from Equador, *A. balaoanum* is a prolific grower. The billowy, paper-thin leaves of this incredible *Anthurium* are truly a sight to behold, especially at maturity. Indoors, this climber requires the support of a totem and plenty of humidity to thrive.

Anthurium andraeanum

Anthurium scandens

COMMON NAME PEARL LACELEAF

Named for the clusters of white or sometimes light lavender pearl-esque berries it produces, the *Anthurium scandens* is a climbing vine with fleshy stems and glossy leaves.

CARE LEVEL
novice

LIGHT
bright, indirect

WATER
moderate–high

SOIL
well-draining

HUMIDITY
medium

PROPAGATION
division

GROWTH HABIT
climbing

POSITION
tabletop

TOXICITY
toxic

Native to Central and South America, the pearl laceleaf is widespread in the wild and grows at a variety of altitudes, but almost always in moist tropical conditions, so take cues from its homelands and keep your plant well misted. As an epiphytic plant, it will benefit from an orchid potting mix, which the roots can attach themselves to. It thrives in bright, indirect light, but be sure to avoid any harsh direct sunrays.

Commercially, most anthuriums are propagated by tissue culture, but at home division or stem cuttings work best. All *Anthurium* are toxic to pets and the pearl laceleaf can also irritate our skin and eyes, so take care when handling these dramatic beauties!

A. scandens needs to be staked once it grows to size, and it will then sit happily on a tabletop from where you can best enjoy the berries, but only with your eyes.

Anthurium veitchii

All hail his royal majesty, the king anthurium! Endemic to the Colombian rainforest, this plant, with its large, dramatically corrugated glossy leaves that can grow to over one metre (3 ft, 3 in), truly reigns supreme.

CARE LEVEL
green thumb

LIGHT
bright, indirect

WATER
moderate

SOIL
well-draining +
moisture-retaining

HUMIDITY
high

PROPAGATION
stem cuttings

GROWTH HABIT
climbing

POSITION
bookshelf or stand

TOXICITY
toxic

The incredible foliage is certainly some of the more impressive we have seen, with large flat leaves that face the sun like thin shields or long flags dangling from their stems. Delicate when young, the leaves become more resilient with age; however, they never really grow to like direct sun, so please keep this regal beauty away from harsh rays.

Anthurium veitchii enjoys a moist but well-draining soil – an orchid potting mix works best. The soil needs to stay relatively moist during the warmer months, but you can back right off in winter. Feed with half-strength liquid fertiliser once or twice a month in spring and summer. It's worth investing in a good-quality fertiliser and avoiding slow-release varieties, which can contribute to salt build-up that can damage your plant's roots.

Be sure to mist daily or set up a pebble and water-filled saucer, because these guys like it humid. Anthuriums are particularly sensitive to cold draughts, so make sure to protect your plant in winter, and keep it clear of heaters and air-conditioning units. Because the king anthurium naturally finds itself dangling from tree crevices, a high shelf or plant stand makes the premium spot to show off this particularly special plant.

Anthurium vittarifolium

COMMON NAME STRAP LEAF ANTHURIUM

Anthurium vittarifolium is a type of strap leaf anthurium sporting long sword-like leaves that dangle daintily from its centre.

CARE LEVEL
novice

LIGHT
bright, indirect

WATER
moderate–high

SOIL
moisture-retaining

HUMIDITY
high

PROPAGATION
division

GROWTH HABIT
trailing

POSITION
bookshelf or stand

TOXICITY
toxic

In the wild, these leaves can grow to an impressive 2.5 metres (8 ft) tall, and the unusual shape of the mature plant makes for a very striking addition to any jungle collection. The berries that are produced post flowering on the small and inconsequential inflorescence are also worth a mention for their bright pops of pink and purple colouring.

Native to Colombia, *A. vittarifolium* is a jungle-dwelling hemi-epiphytic plant that does not appreciate direct sun, so indoors it's best to keep it in a spot with lots of bright, indirect light. A potting mix with some additional sphagnum moss can help retain precious moisture, and only allow the top layer of soil to dry out before watering again – roughly once a week should do the trick, but always test the soil with your finger first. Spritz regularly, and keep your plant in a warm spot away from cool draughts.

If you are lucky enough to own one of these plants, be sure to show off its dramatic leaf display in a hanging pot or atop a plant stand.

Anthurium warocqueanum

COMMON NAME QUEEN ANTHURIUM

Beloved by plant collectors the world over, *Anthurium warocqueanum* has large lance-shaped leaves with silver veins that get more pronounced with age, and that pop against its moody velutinous surface.

CARE LEVEL
green thumb

LIGHT
bright, indirect

WATER
moderate–high

SOIL
well-draining

HUMIDITY
high

PROPAGATION
division

GROWTH HABIT
climbing

POSITION
bookshelf or stand

TOXICITY
toxic

These leaves, which grow up to 90 cm (3 ft) indoors, can reach an incredible 2 metres (6 ft, 6 in) outside. According to growers of this plant, it is highly variable, with supposed cultivars often proving to be simply natural variations of the same species.

Anthurium warocqueanum enjoys a moist but never soggy environment. An orchid potting mix, combined with moss wrapped around the base of the trunk, will help to mimic its natural epiphytic home. It will benefit from a half-strength fertiliser once a month during the warmer seasons.

The queen anthurium is serious plant royalty, so be sure to display it as such. It can be wall-mounted or give it pride of place on a plant stand or prominent shelf.

Dioscorea

Named after the ancient Greek physician and botanist Dioscorides, *Dioscorea* is a genus of more than 600 species of flowering plants in the Dioscoreaceae family. Generally tuberous, woody-stemmed climbing vines that grow from 2–12 metres (6 ft, 6 in–40 ft) tall, they are native to many tropical and some temperate regions of the world. Their leaves are mostly heart-shaped and alternately arranged on their spiralling vines.

Several species, known as yams, are valued as agricultural crops and their large tubers are an important food source in tropical regions of South America, Asia, Africa and Oceania. Although mainly toxic when raw, they are made edible by different methods of preparation and cooking. Medicinally, the toxin steroidal saponins, found in many species of *Dioscorea*, can be converted into steroid hormones. A number of *Dioscorea*, including the elephant's foot (*Dioscorea sylvatica*; see page 182) and the ornamental yam (*Dioscorea dodecaneura*; see page 181) are beautifully suited to houseplant life.

Dioscorea dodecaneura

COMMON NAME ORNAMENTAL YAM

A rare stunner, the ornamental yam is a dramatic vine hailing from Ecuador and Brazil with intricate and unusual variegation on its heart-shaped foliage.

CARE LEVEL
green thumb

LIGHT
bright, indirect +
full sun

WATER
moderate–high

SOIL
well-draining

HUMIDITY
medium

PROPAGATION
division

GROWTH HABIT
climbing + trailing

POSITION
bookshelf or stand

TOXICITY
pet friendly

A living artwork, *Dioscorea dodecaneura*'s deep green leaves, which increase in size as the plant matures, are randomly mottled with maroon and black, with silver veining and rich-pinkish purple undersides.

Quirkily, the ornamental yam twines in a counter-clockwise direction, a unique vining action that allows it to gently grow its way upwards despite its incredibly dainty stems. In addition to its gorgeous foliage, its flowers, which bloom in drooping clusters, are small, white and perfumed. You are unlikely to witness these blooms indoors but with leaves this good, you won't miss them.

This plant needs plenty of light. It will appreciate at least four hours of direct gentle morning or late afternoon sunlight. Lots of bright, indirect light will also be tolerated. The ornamental yam is a thirsty tropical plant that needs watering as soon as the top 5 cm (2 in) of soil has dried out in spring and summer, but if temperatures drop dramatically in winter it can go dormant, dying back to its tuberous base. When this happens, stop watering and allow the potting mix to dry out completely between drinks. You can begin watering again in spring when its growth cycle recommences.

Dioscorea sylvatica

COMMON NAME **ELEPHANT'S FOOT YAM**

The elephant's foot yam is a delicately twining herb with stems growing from a tuberous caudex marked with net-like patterning.

CARE LEVEL
novice

LIGHT
bright, indirect

WATER
moderate

SOIL
coarse + sandy

HUMIDITY
low

PROPAGATION
stem cutting

GROWTH HABIT
climbing

POSITION
bookshelf or stand

TOXICITY
toxic

With its vigorous climbing stems, which can grow up to 4–5 metres (13–16 ft) in a season and look fantastic trained around a wire hoop in a pot, *Dioscorea sylvatica* makes an easy and stunningly unusual houseplant.

The elephant's foot yam is native to Zambia, Mozambique, Zimbabwe, Eswatini (formerly Swaziland) and South Africa where it grows slowly in a variety of evenly moist wooded areas. Sadly there has been a significant population decline in the wild due to human activity, and it is now considered a vulnerable species.

When cultivated indoors, this plant's water needs are moderate during a growth phase but will need to be reduced when the tuber is dormant in summer. It will begin to shoot again come autumn, and you can recommence watering once you see signs of fresh growth. It is also not completely unusual for plants to ignore prescribed growing seasons and continue growing long into their rest period. The elephant's foot yam may send up new vines earlier than expected, and for this reason it is best to respond to the plant rather than adhering to any hard and fast rules. This plant can be propagated via stem cutting or by sowing their seeds. Plant the seeds 5 mm (¼ in) deep into well-draining seed-raising potting mix and keep in a warm and bright, indirectly lit spot.

Cremanthodium

Cremanthodium is a genus of around 50 flowering plants in the Daisy or Asteraceae family. Certainly one of the lesser known genera, they are a group of rather obscure plants hailing from the alpine regions of Nepal and China. When grown outside, they require cool summer temperatures and evenly moist soil, but in winter they need to be protected from getting soggy feet – they even enjoy a covering of snow! Kept indoors, they are best grown in fertile, moist soil with plenty of bright light including some direct sun.

CARE LEVEL
novice

LIGHT
bright, indirect–
full sun

WATER
moderate–high

SOIL
well-draining

HUMIDITY
medium

PROPAGATION
division

GROWTH HABIT
clumping

POSITION
floor + covered
balcony

TOXICITY
toxic

Cremanthodium reniforme

COMMON NAME **TRACTOR SEAT PLANT Syn:** *Ligularia reniformis*

The huge, glossy, kidney-shaped leaves of the *Cremanthodium reniforme* (or tractor seat plant as it is commonly known) are truly spectacular, and the addition of this sculptural plant to an indoor space or sheltered balcony is sure to invite admiration. Even better, this distinctive beauty is hardy and easy to grow in the right, moist conditions.

This versatile plant can handle a variety of positions from full sun to bright, indirect light, but it will need to be protected from harsh afternoon rays. *C. reniforme* is a clump-forming plant that can grow up to one metre (3 ft, 3 in) high and wide. Planted in a container, it is likely to stay more compact, which suits an indoor environment. The tractor seat plant can become

dormant in winter, so don't panic if growth comes to a standstill as the weather cools. Keep its well-draining potting mix consistently moist during spring and summer but but taper off come autumn.

It's worth noting that *C. reniforme* was previously known as *Ligularia reniformis* within the *Ligularia* genus (commonly known as leopard plants for their yellow or orange flower heads with brown or yellow centres that resemble big cat markings). Although no longer classified as a *Ligularia,* in an outdoor environment the tractor seat plant will produce the yellow-orange daisy-like flowers for which its previous genus is known. Indoors it is unlikely to flower but the lovely leaves alone are more than enough to satisfy.

specimen *Peperomia obtusifolia* 'variegata'

Peperomia

Commonly referred to as radiator plants for their appreciation of warm temperatures, this prolific genus has over 1500 recorded species, making it the second largest within the Piperaceae family. This genus was first formally described in 1794 by Spanish botanists Hipólito Ruiz López and José Antonio Pavón.

Peperomia are native to many tropical and sub-tropical regions, mainly in Central America and northern South America, with a few species even making their way to Africa and Australia. Grown for their attractive and vibrant foliage that encompasses a variety of colours, shapes and textures, one thing these plants have in common is their compact nature, making them ideal plants for apartment dwellers. They make great entry-level houseplants, as they're relatively low maintenance and pest resistant. Some species are more succulent than others, so it's important to note their specific care requirements. In the wild, *Peperomia* grow on the rainforest floor, often epiphytically on pieces of rotten wood. Their inflorescence appears as conical spikes, protruding above the leaf layer.

Peperomia argyreia

COMMON NAME WATERMELON PEPEROMIA

As with most *Peperomia*, it's definitely all about the foliage with this pretty plant. The thick succulent ovate leaves are distinctly marked with silver patterns just like those of a watermelon rind, with deep red petioles to match. Unsurprisingly, this is one of the most popular species of *Peperomia* out there.

CARE LEVEL
green thumb

LIGHT
bright, indirect

WATER
moderate

SOIL
well-draining

HUMIDITY
low

PROPAGATION
stem + leaf cuttings

GROWTH HABIT
clumping

POSITION
tabletop

TOXICITY
pet friendly

Native to South America, this beauty generally doesn't reach heights of more than 20 cm (8 in), but its leaves can sometimes grow as big as the palm of your hand. This semi-succulent foliage means that it doesn't like to be overwatered, and it can be particularly prone to root rot if its home is continuously moist. Be sure to only water once the first 5 cm (2 in) of potting mix has dried out, and a little less in winter when light and ambient temperatures drop.

The watermelon peperomia is definitely opposed to the cold, so it's best kept coddled among other plants and away from draughts and air-conditioning units. Its blooms are relatively insignificant and some growers cut off the small spiky inflorescence in order to encourage leaf growth, for which the plants are generally favoured. Either way, be sure to cut off the flowers once they are spent, along any dead leaves that appear.

Watermelon peperomia like bright, indirect light (no harsh afternoon rays, please) and will benefit from a monthly half-strength liquid fertiliser in spring and summer.

Peperomia caperata

COMMON NAME EMERALD RIPPLE PEPEROMIA

Hailing from the Brazilian rainforest, *Peperomia caperata* has heart-shaped, semi-succulent leaves with a deeply ridged texture. There are many cultivars of this species, including the luna red, mottled variegata and deep green emerald ripple (pictured here), all of which stay petite in size.

CARE LEVEL
novice

LIGHT
bright, indirect

WATER
low–moderate

SOIL
well-draining

HUMIDITY
low

PROPAGATION
stem + leaf cuttings

GROWTH HABIT
clumping

POSITION
tabletop

TOXICITY
pet friendly

Be particularly careful not to overwater this plant, especially in the cooler months, as it will inevitably lead to root rot. Wilting leaves can be either a sign of dehydration or over-watering (confusing we know!). If you notice your plant exhibiting these signs, take stock: if it's wilting after a recent watering, pull back on how much water you're giving your plant, but if it's been a while between drinks it's probably ready to be watered.

The emerald ripple peperomia thrives in bright, indirect light, but it will happily live in slightly lower-light conditions, too.

Because of the semi-succulent nature of the leaves, it doesn't require high levels of humidity – a spritz here and there will suffice. Generally, these plants don't grow large enough to require repotting, and actually prefer being slightly root-bound, but their potting mix will need a half-strength fertiliser top-up every fortnight or so during the warmer seasons.

Because of its small size this peperomia makes a great terrarium plant, and it also does well in office spaces because of its tolerance of fluorescent lighting, as long as it's consistent.

Peperomia obtusifolia

BABY RUBBER PLANT

Native to the Caribbean, Florida and Mexico, *Peperomia obtusifolia* has deep green, waxy, semi-succulent leaves and an easy-going disposition. It's a bushy upright plant that grows to a manageable 25 cm (10 in) high and wide, with simple white flower spikes that appear from spring to autumn.

CARE LEVEL
novice

LIGHT
bright, indirect

WATER
low–moderate

SOIL
well-draining

HUMIDITY
medium

PROPAGATION
leaf + stem cuttings

GROWTH HABIT
clumping

POSITION
tabletop

TOXICITY
pet friendly

There are a few cultivars of this species, from the grey-green, gold and ivory tones of the *Peperomia obtusifolia* 'albo-marginata' to the whiter and brighter green shades of the *Peperomia obtusifolia* 'variegata'. The variegated plants require more light than their non-variegated cousins, but for both, bright, indirect light, with a little direct gentle morning sun, is best.

Because it has a shallow root system, the baby rubber plant won't require regular repotting, but when you do, make sure you only increase the pot size just slightly; otherwise, like all peperomias, the excess potting mix will risk the plant's root system becoming waterlogged and rotten. On this note, it only needs a low to moderate amount of water, so make sure that half the potting mix has dried out before watering again, and water even more sparingly in winter.

Fertilise monthly with a half-strength liquid fertiliser, and pinch off leggy growth to encourage a more bushy appearance. Better yet, take cuttings from your prunings and propagate your plant. A single leaf with a small stem attached will do. Just allow the cutting to dry out for a day before inserting into fresh potting mix and keeping warm until it roots.

Peperomia obtusifolia 'variegata'

Peperomia turboensis

This dainty peperomia has teardrop-shaped, dark grey leaves with metallic silver markings and burgundy undersides. It's native to tropical South America and loves a little humidity. In the wild, it grows both terrestrially and epiphytically and remains quite small, making it a perfect plant for terrariums.

Peperomia polybotrya

COMMON NAME **RAINDROP PEPEROMIA**

Named for its raindrop-shaped glossy green leaves, the raindrop, or coin-leaf, peperomia is one of the larger species within the *Peperomia* genus, reaching not-so lofty heights of about 30 cm (12 in).

CARE LEVEL
novice

LIGHT
bright, indirect

WATER
low—moderate

SOIL
well-draining

HUMIDITY
medium

PROPAGATION
leaf + stem cuttings

GROWTH HABIT
clumping

POSITION
tabletop

TOXICITY
pet friendly

Native to tropical South America, the raindrop peperomia grows epiphytically in the wild, without an extensive root structure. The semi-succulent leaves and stems store water well, so indoors it only requires a low to moderate amount of water, letting the majority of the soil dry out between drinks.

Small inflorescence produce fleeting, sweet-smelling flowers, which can be snipped off at the base once they are spent. Because of its semi-succulent nature, the raindrop peperomia doesn't have high humidity needs, but do try and mimic its natural tropical environment with a semi-regular spritz, ensuring there is adequate air flow so the leaves and soil don't stay damp.

Peperomia polybotrya is a slow grower, but like most *Peperomia*, it propagates easily via leaf and stem cuttings. In spring, neatly cut a leaf with some petiole attached and allow to dry out for 24 hours before gently sticking into potting mix, petiole end in. Although unlikely to need regular repotting, raindrop peperomias tend to clump (either due to multiple buried nodes or from tissue culture), so the plant will widen over time, with extra branches expanding from the base. For optimal growth, fertilise your plant with half-strength, well-balanced liquid fertiliser every month or so during spring and summer, but lay off during autumn and winter.

Peperomia scandens

COMMON NAME CUPID PEPEROMIA

With small, waxy, heart-shaped leaves, the cupid peperomia will make his way straight into your heart with some seriously low-fuss ways.

CARE LEVEL
novice

LIGHT
bright, indirect

WATER
low–moderate

SOIL
well-draining

HUMIDITY
low

PROPAGATION
stem cutting

GROWTH HABIT
trailing

POSITION
bookshelf or stand

TOXICITY
pet friendly

The foliage of the *Peperomia scandens* 'variegata' (pictured here) boasts a light green centre, decorated with a pleasing cream outline setting it apart from the plainer but no less lovely *Peperomia scandens*. The stems of this peperomia can reach 90 cm (3 ft) in length and will trail attractively over the pot's edge, making it, along with the *Peperomia polybotrya*, one of the larger peperomias. Native to tropical Mexico and South America, this plant grows epiphytically in the wild, and is beautifully low maintenance indoors.

The cupid peperomia's fleshy leaves and shallow root system mean that it doesn't require lots of water, so always ensure half the soil dries out between drinks. And you can rest easy as it's relatively forgiving if you're a bit forgetful on the watering front. The 'variegata' will require a little more light to maintain those cultivated patterns, but bright light, with some direct gentle morning rays, will suit both plants, and they will also tolerate lower-light conditions if they must. Neither plant likes the cold, preferring warm and somewhat humid environments, but the natural humidity of your home should be adequate. Fertilise once a month with a liquid fertiliser during the warmer growing seasons.

Homalomena

Growing in abundance in the tropical climes of Colombia, Costa Rica and the rainforest floors of Southern Asia and east to Melanesia, *Homalomena* is a genus of flowering plants within the Araceae family. Their foliage and stems range from deep greens to reds, burgundies and copper tones. Commonly collectively known as the queen of hearts or shield plant for their matte, heart-shaped leaves that can grow up to 30 cm (12 in) in ideal conditions, they are clump-forming evergreen perennials producing thin finger-like petal-less blooms.

Although there are a multitude of species of *Homalomena*, few are available commercially as indoor plants and it is the cultivars and hybrids that are grown for their ease of care and attractive foliage that make up the majority of the *Homalomena* houseplant market.

CARE LEVEL
novice

LIGHT
bright, indirect

WATER
moderate

SOIL
well-draining

HUMIDITY
medium–high

PROPAGATION
division

GROWTH HABIT
clumping

POSITION
tabletop

TOXICITY
toxic

Homalomena rubescens 'Maggie'

COMMON NAME QUEEN OF HEARTS

Homalomena rubescens 'Maggie' is a cultivar grown for its jungle vibes and easy-care M.O. A tropical aroid, it is elevated by deep red stems from which its gorgeous glossy foliage extends. Its large heart-shaped leaves are beautifully textured with deep ridges and, what's more, they were even recognised in the NASA Clean Air Study for their excellent air-purification abilities.

As a fellow member of the Araceae family, care of the *Homalomena rubescens* 'Maggie' is similar to that of its close relative, *Philodendron*. Bright, indirect light is best and moderate humidity requirements means it is well suited to the home environment, as long as it's kept clear of heaters and coolers. Higher levels of humidity will not go unappreciated, so feel free to mist at will, ensuring air ventilation is also plentiful. Water thoroughly when the top 2.5 cm (1 in) of its well-draining potting mix is dry.

'Maggie' is a steady grower, but it doesn't require frequent repotting, which makes for wonderfully effortless care. A clumping growth habit lends this *Homalomena* to a position on a tabletop or bench, saving precious floor space in small rooms.

Scindapsus

Scindapsus is a genus of around 35 species of evergreen perennials with vining habits in the Araceae family. Native to Southeast Asia, New Guinea, Queensland and a few western Pacific Islands, they are typically grown for their lovely foliage. A number of variegated varieties and cultivars exist, including *Scindapsus pictus* var. *argyraeus* or satin vine (see opposite), which is much adored for its ease of growth indoors.

Not easily distinguishable from *Epipremnum* (see page 54) and, therefore, commonly (but incorrectly) known as pothos, the biggest difference between the two genera is their seeds. *Scindapsus* produce only one kidney-shaped seed while *Epipremnum* produces multiple seeds.

CARE LEVEL
novice

LIGHT
bright, indirect

WATER
moderate

SOIL
well-draining

HUMIDITY
medium

PROPAGATION
stem cuttings

GROWTH HABIT
trailing

POSITION
bookshelf or stand

TOXICITY
toxic

Scindapsus pictus var. argyraeus

COMMON NAME SATIN VINE

Glorious trailing foliage in a sumptuous matte green that's daintily speckled with silver blotches helps make the satin vine one seriously spectacular indoor plant. Native to much of South and Southeast Asia, in the wild the satin vine climbs up tree trunks and ambles along the ground reaching up to 3 metres (10 ft) in length. Indoors, it trails beautifully from a hanging planter, but looks equally fab dangling down from a high shelf.

The epithet *pictus* means 'painted', and refers to the delicate silver variegation on the leaves. As with all variegated plants, the mutation will be stronger in ideal light conditions, and the satin vine likes plenty of bright, indirect light. It will tolerate lower-light conditions, but generally to the detriment of its beautiful markings.

Plant in well-draining soil and water deeply, allowing the top 2–5 cm (¾–2 in) of the potting mix to dry out between drinks. Although unfussy, *S. pictus* does not enjoy having wet feet, and the appearance of yellowing leaves can indicate an over-watered plant. The satin vine enjoys being pruned and cuttings can be easily propagated in water. Once the roots reach 8–10 cm (3¼–4 in) it is ready for planting, either back in with the mother plant or into a new pot.

S. pictus is delightfully pest resistant, and as long as you avoid over-watering it should stay pest free.

specimen *Alocasia zebrina*

Alocasia

Hailing from tropical and subtropical Asia and eastern Australia, there are currently 80 accepted species of *Alocasia*. With mostly broad, showy leaves, from the velutinous texture of the *Alocasia reginula* (black velvet alocasia; see page 211), to the glossy zig-zagged edge of the *Alocasia sanderiana* (kris plant; see page 212), these plants are certainly dramatic (and a little needy!). Not to be confused with the closely allied genus *Colocasia*, alocasias are either rhizomatous or tuberous and, like other aroids, they have generally unremarkable flowers that grow on a spathe and spadix. While they do provide some uses in the medical world, alocasias are generally highly toxic and should be kept out of reach of pesky pets and curious kids.

Alocasia clypeolata

COMMON NAME GREEN SHIELD ALOCASIA

With large, leathery, lime green leaves lined with prominent dark veins that become almost black as the plant ages, the *Alocasia clypeolata* is a rare and unusual beauty.

CARE LEVEL
green thumb

LIGHT
bright, indirect

WATER
moderate–high

SOIL
well-draining +
moisture-retaining

HUMIDITY
high

PROPAGATION
division + offsets

GROWTH HABIT
clumping

POSITION
floor

TOXICITY
toxic

This plant, which is an elephant ear species, hails from the Philippines and enjoys lots of warmth and humidity. Its leaves can grow 25 cm (10 in) long, while the whole plant can reach approximately 1.2 metres (4 ft) high and wide. A fast grower in summer, it will need consistently moist soil during the warmer seasons, allowing only the top layer to dry out between drinks. Keep in mind that this special *Alocasia* will likely become semi-dormant in winter, so you should slow your watering schedule; just be sure not to totally forget about your houseplant.

Green shield alocasia will appreciate a monthly feed in spring and summer with a half-strength liquid fertiliser. Its growth will slow if it becomes root bound, so if you want a large, healthy plant, repot it every year or two. This is also a great time to propagate. Because of their clumping nature, you can easily divide the root system into two or simply cut off and repot any baby plants that have appeared around the base.

Alocasia macrorrhizos

COMMON NAME GIANT TARO

With leaves big enough to be used as an umbrella in a tropical downpour, the *Alocasia macrorrhizos* can grow to heights of 3 metres (10 ft). This giant plant will stay a more manageable size indoors, but be sure to place it in a spot where it will have some room to grow.

CARE LEVEL
green thumb

LIGHT
bright, indirect

WATER
moderate–high

SOIL
well-draining

HUMIDITY
medium–high

PROPAGATION
division + offsets

GROWTH HABIT
clumping

POSITION
covered balcony

TOXICITY
toxic

Its glossy, emerald green leaves with prominent veins and ruffled edges point upwards, which is the opposite of its similar-looking relation *Colocasia esculenta*, whose leaves droop downwards.

Native to the rainforests of Borneo, Southeast Asia and Queensland, it is also cultivated in many parts of the Pacific Islands. Parts of the plant are edible if cooked very thoroughly, but generally this plant is considered highly toxic.

The giant taro will feel right at home on a covered balcony; just be sure to keep its leaves away from harsh afternoon rays and windy conditions, as they are easily scorched and torn. This plant likes a rich, moist potting mix, so water regularly, ensuring that only the top layer of soil dries out, and fertilise once a month during the warmer growing seasons (although cut right back on food and water during winter). *Alocasia macrorrhizos'* big leaves will need to be cleaned regularly with a damp cloth or delicate leaf brush.

The cultivar 'stingray' (pictured here), has unusual-shaped leaves that curl inwards and a tip that tapers into a long thin tail like its marine counterpart. The patterned stems are similar to the *Alocasia zebrina*. It requires a little more humidity than the standard *macrorrhizos*, so we recommend keeping this plant on a water-filled pebble tray, and avoid spritzing the leaves directly, unless it's in a well-ventilated spot.

Alocasia macrorrhizos 'stingray'

Alocasia reginula

COMMON NAME BLACK VELVET ALOCASIA

One of the sweeter, smaller alocasias going around, this little black beauty has velutinous leaves lined with silvery veins. The black velvet alocasia is part of a special and small gang of plants with near-black colouring. It joins the likes of *Zamioculcas zamiifolia* 'raven' and *Colocasia esculenta* 'black magic' in this seductively selective crew.

CARE LEVEL
green thumb

LIGHT
bright, indirect

WATER
moderate

SOIL
well-draining

HUMIDITY
medium

PROPAGATION
offsets + plantlets

GROWTH HABIT
clumping

POSITION
tabletop

TOXICITY
toxic

Native to Southeast Asia, the *Alocasia reginula* grows terrestrially on the jungle floor. Its leaves feel slightly fleshier than those of its relatives, having evolved to tolerate slightly drier conditions. As such, it requires a little less water than other alocasias, and it is best suited to being watered deeply, but infrequently, allowing at least 5 cm (2 in) of soil to dry out between drinks. Good ventilation is key, so ensure you crack a window and don't jam it too closely among your other plants.

While the black velvet alocasia can grow to 60 cm (2 ft) tall in perfect conditions, it will more likely stay a squat 20 cm (8 in) indoors. It doesn't need to be repotted regularly, but when you do, make sure you only increase your pot size slightly; otherwise you risk the roots becoming waterlogged through excess potting mix. Treat this beauty right and she will reward you with gorgeous foliage year after year.

Alocasia sanderiana

COMMON NAME **KRIS PLANT**

This boldly patterned plant is endemic to parts of the Philippines, and gathers its common name from the wavy-edged Filipino sword, the kalis or kris dagger.

CARE LEVEL
green thumb

LIGHT
bright, indirect

WATER
moderate–high

SOIL
well-draining

HUMIDITY
medium

PROPAGATION
division + offsets

GROWTH HABIT
clumping

POSITION
tabletop

TOXICITY
toxic

The kris plant can grow to 2 metres (6 ft, 6 in) tall in the wild, but probably won't reach such lofty heights indoors. It has visually insignificant creamy white inflorescence, but some seriously dramatic foliage that will add a tropical vibe to any plant collection. Large, glossy, dark green v-shaped leaves, which can reach impressive lengths of 40 cm (16 in), are lined with silvery white veins and edging and a reddish underside. Although a popular houseplant, in the wild this plant is sadly considered critically endangered.

Where possible, use distilled water on your kris plant, making sure it stays relatively moist in summer, but allow the soil to dry out more substantially in winter, when its growth slows down. It will benefit from a fortnightly half-strength fertiliser in spring and summer, but once again, give your plant a rest during the colder seasons.

Like many alocasias, the kris plant can be prone to pests, so be sure to stay on top of its care needs, as prevention is always better than cure. Ensure that is in a moderately warm and humid environment (it is a tropical plant, after all) and regularly wipe down the leaves with a damp cloth, or give the plant a gentle shower, to remove any dust build-up. This regular attention gives you a good opportunity to inspect for pests and apply an eco-oil if required.

Alocasia zebrina

ZEBRA ALOCASIA

A very dainty alocasia indeed, the *Alocasia zebrina* has upright arrow-shaped leaves that extend from fantastically striped stems.

CARE LEVEL
expert

LIGHT
bright, indirect

WATER
moderate

SOIL
well-draining

HUMIDITY
medium–high

PROPAGATION
division + offsets + plantlets

GROWTH HABIT
upright

POSITION
tabletop

TOXICITY
toxic

The zebra alocasia can be a little finicky to care for, and finding the perfect environment can take a little experimentation, but once you find the sweet spot, (that's as close to its origins in tropical Southeast Asia as possible), it will reward you handsomely.

This plant likes high humidity and spritzing the leaves will certainly help, but be sure to provide adequate ventilation so that water isn't left sitting for long periods on the foliage. Placing your plant on a water-filled pebble tray can also help increase ambient moisture. When watering, allow the first 5 cm (2 in) of potting mix to dry out between drinks. In terms of light, bright, indirect is best, and it will also enjoy some gentle morning rays.

Alocasia zebrina can grow to heights of 90 cm (3 ft), but it is likely to go dormant if temperatures consistently drop below 15°C (59°F). If this happens the leaves will yellow and drop, but don't worry; simply cut off any dead stems with clean sharp secateurs, water sparingly and eliminate fertiliser, and it will bounce back once warmer weather returns.

Propagate this plant via division of the rhizome, or by replanting its little offsets. Like a lot of alocasias, the divisions can live happily in a jar of water for a period of time, as long as just the roots (not the bulb) are submerged. It makes for quite a sight to see the tangle of roots below the boldly striped stems and lush leaves.

There is also an elusive variegated cultivar of the *A. zebrina*. If you manage to get your hands on one, be sure to treasure it wholly.

Colocasia

Originally from Southeast Asia and the Indian subcontinent, these wonderfully tropical plants are widely cultivated in many regions of the world for their edible tubers, known as taro. Despite their edible nature, be mindful that these plants are toxic if eaten raw. They must be fermented, soaked or cooked to rid them of the irritant they produce to help deter animals from eating them.

Colocasia's soft green leaves – reminiscent of shields or elephant ears (from which the genus gets its common name) – can grow very large, and in some species, such as *Colocasia gigantea*, they can reach up to 1.5 metres (4 ft, 9 in). Similar in some respects to their close relative *Alocasia* (see page 205), *Colocasia* can be identified by their horizontal or downwards-drooping leaves (as opposed to the upward-pointing leaves of *Alocasia*). Although *Colocasia* is a small genus of around only 10 species, there are many vibrant cultivars, such as the black mottled *Colocasia esculenta* 'mojito' and the red-stemmed *Colocasia esculenta* 'rhubarb'.

CARE LEVEL
green thumb

LIGHT
bright, indirect–
full sun

WATER
moderate–high

SOIL
moisture-retaining

HUMIDITY
moderate

PROPAGATION
division

GROWTH HABIT
clumping

POSITION
covered balcony

TOXICITY
toxic

Colocasia esculenta

COMMON NAME **ELEPHANT EAR**

One of the most common species within the *Colocasia* genus, *C. esculenta* has large bright green leaves that can grow 40 cm (16 in) long. Like most *Colocasia*, the elephant ear thrives in moisture-rich soil and can even be grown aquatically. Water regularly, ensuring that only the top 5 cm (2 in) of potting mix dries out between drinks. It need lots of bright, direct and indirect light, but avoid uber-harsh direct afternoon rays that may burn the leaves. In winter, if temperatures drop dramatically, growth will slow or enter a short dormancy period. During this time, water less frequently until warmer weather returns.

Colocasia are hungry plants, so feed them regularly during the warmer seasons. New leaves will invariably replace the old, so be sure to chop off any dead foliage at the base of the stem with sharp secateurs to keep your plant tidy. Clean the leaves in the shower or wipe with a damp cloth if your plant is too big to lug around. It can be prone to spider mites and other pests, so regularly check for signs of invasion.

If you have a larger specimen, be sure to place it in an equally large pot. *Colocasia* can get top heavy and you don't want your elephant ear tipping over. Also keep in mind that this plant has a spreading growth habit and in an outdoor environment it has a propensity to get out of hand. In the US it is considered an invasive species, while in Australia it can grow like weeds, so keep your elephant ear in a pot or in a closed environment, such as a pond.

Chlorophytum

Native to tropical and subtropical regions of Africa, Asia and Australia, *Chlorophytum* is a genus of around 150 species of flowering plants in the Asparagaceae family. The most common *Chlorophytum* grown as an ornamental houseplant is undoubtedly the spider plant (*Chlorophytum comosum*), named for the plantlets it produces on long arching stems that dangle like baby spiders.

A genus of generally petite, evergreen herbs, *Chlorophytum* can grow to around 60 cm (2 ft) tall. Their long, narrow leaves sprout from a central point at the base of the plant and they have fleshy, tuberous roots with several species rhizomatous.

CARE LEVEL
novice

LIGHT
low–moderate

WATER
moderate

SOIL
well-draining

HUMIDITY
medium

PROPAGATION
plantlets + offsets

GROWTH HABIT
clumping + trailing

POSITION
bookshelf or stand

TOXICITY
pet friendly

Chlorophytum comosum

COMMON NAME **SPIDER PLANT**

One of the houseplants du jour in the 1970s, the popularity of the spider plant has waxed and waned over the years. Thankfully, as with most things, it has come back into fashion so we can once again get our hands on this lush, fast-growing and incredibly low-maintenance houseplant. Originally from South Africa, *Chlorophytum comosum* made its way into European homes in the mid-19th century. While wild specimens growing in subtropical and tropical regions feature purely green foliage, cultivars such as *Chlorophytum comosum* 'vittatum' have a broad white stripe down the centre of their leaves. For even more quirk, the *Chlorophytum comosum* 'Bonnie' is the curly cousin of this stalwart, and she's got all the ease of the common variety but with some added pizzazz.

Because spider plants are so unfussy they can manage in low light (although growth will be slowed) and are often placed in bathrooms. Unfortunately for them it means that they are sometimes referred to, rather unglamorously, as the toilet plant, but don't let that put you off.

Producing offsets or baby spiders that dangle elegantly from the mother plant, *C. comosum* is wonderfully easy to propagate and you will find your collection multiplying in no time. This is a plant that needs very little fertiliser, and too much can impede the production of offsets. Keep its well-draining potting mix evenly moist, but avoid overwatering or you'll end up with brown leaves and waterlogged roots. An excess of fluoride in tap water can also cause the leaf tips to brown, so use distilled water when you can.

Chlorophytum comosum 'Bonnie'

Cissus

With a name derived from the Greek word *kissos*, meaning 'ivy', *Cissus* is a genus of about 350 species of woody vines in the Vitaceae family. *Cissus* grow the world over, though the majority are found in tropical climates. Many species sport fleshy and somewhat succulent leaves.

At least a dozen species in this genus are used in traditional medicines. In Australia, *Cissus hypoglauca* is made into a remedy for sore throats while in Southeast Asia *Cissus quadrangularis* is used to promote fracture healing. A number of these plants are also cultivated for the garden, while some, such as *Cissus rhombifolia* (grape ivy; see opposite) and *Cissus antarctica* (kangaroo vine), are grown as popular indoor plants.

CARE LEVEL
novice

LIGHT
low–moderate

WATER
moderate

SOIL
well-draining

HUMIDITY
medium

PROPAGATION
stem cuttings

GROWTH HABIT
trailing

POSITION
bookshelf or stand

TOXICITY
toxic

Cissus rhombifolia

COMMON NAME GRAPE IVY

Although this plant looks somewhat like an ivy (*Hedera* genus), *Cissus rhombifolia* is not a true ivy at all. Rather, it belongs to the other part of its common name and is actually a member of the grape family, with foliage and dark berries that are reminiscent of the wine-making grapevine.

Of all the species of *Cissus*, the grape ivy is one of the most tolerant of indoor growing conditions. In the wild – namely Venezuela – this tropical vine trails in abundance reaching up to 3 metres (10 ft) long. Indoors, it works beautifully on a shelf or stand where its vining foliage is allowed to cascade, but can also be trained up a textured totem or trellis for upwards growth.

Less is definitely more when it comes to caring for this beauty. Although it prefers a spot with lots of bright, indirect light, the grape ivy will also happily live in a lower-light position. In a brighter spot it has moderate water needs, but will require less water the darker its position gets. Either way, be sure to let the top 2–5 cm (¾–2 in) of potting mix dry out between drinks and keep the temperature between 10–28°C (50–82°F), as anything outside this range can impede the growth of the long runners of this trailing plant.

Dischidia

Closely aligned with its sister genus *Hoya* (see page 42), *Dischidia* also belongs to the Apocynaceae family. Unlike hoyas, however, there is some mystery when it comes to the specifics of this particular genus.

There are about 120 species of *Dischidia* that grow epiphytically throughout the tropical regions of Asia, including parts of China and India. They are also native to northeastern Australia. Interestingly, most *Dischidia* grow in arboreal ants' nests, where a number of species have developed symbiotic relationships with the ants. Over time, the plant has modified its leaves to appear inflated, providing the ants with both housing and food storage. In return, the ants provide nutrients from their waste, which collects in the leaves and breaks down.

CARE LEVEL
novice

LIGHT
bright, indirect

WATER
moderate

SOIL
well-draining

HUMIDITY
medium

PROPAGATION
stem cutting

GROWTH HABIT
upright

POSITION
bookshelf or stand

TOXICITY
toxic

Dischidia ovata

COMMON NAME **WATERMELON DISCHIDIA**

With adorably petite, patterned leaves, *Dischidia ovata* is a trailing vine with loads of personality. While its species name references the plant's ovate, or egg-shaped, leaves, it should come as no surprise that its common moniker is inspired by the watermelon rind-esque leaf patterns. The blooms of the watermelon dischidia, which are dainty yellow-green flowers with purplish markings, are less impressive than the leaves, but sweet nonetheless and are likely to appear during the warmer months.

As an epiphyte, *Dischidia ovata* produces roots along its nodes in order to absorb nutrients and water, as well as to secure the plant to its host tree. This makes it decidedly easy to propagate via a stem cutting – simply snip a 10 cm (4 in) section of vine above a node and root in water, sphagnum moss or vermiculite.

The watermelon dischidia is perfectly suited to a hanging basket, mounted on a piece of cork bark or trailing down a bookshelf. However you choose to display it, just ensure that it gets plenty of bright, indirect light. Hailing from the tropics of Southern Asia and northern Australia, it also thrives on high levels of humidity. While the fleshy leaves are good at storing moisture, try to mimic the plant's native environment by giving the leaves a mist every few days.

The plant produces a milky sap that can cause skin irritation for some people, but there is little information available as to its effect on domestic pets. While it is most likely similar to hoyas, which are considered non-toxic, it's probably best to keep your watermelon dischidia away from curious critters.

Dracaena trifasciata and *D. fragrans*

Dracaena

Dracaena is a diverse genus of more than 100 species of plants in the Asparagaceae family. The majority of species are native to Africa, Southern Asia and Australia, but sadly a number of *Dracaena* are listed as endangered as a result of overharvesting and habitat loss.

Several plants within the genus, including the lucky bamboo (*Dracaena braunii*) and the corn plant (*Dracaena fragrans*) are cultivated as houseplants for their striking foliage and easy-going demeanour. They have also proven themselves effective detoxifiers, capable of removing chemicals, such as formaldehyde, from the air indoors. Most species feature narrow sword-shaped leaves, though some resemble trees with crowns of leaves. They produce small flowers that are typically red, yellow or green, and berry-like fruit that rarely appears when kept indoors.

One of the more curious plants is the *Dracaena draco*, which is known for its tendency to ooze a blood-red resin when cut or damaged. Legend says that a hundred-headed dragon was killed and hundreds of trees grew from its red blood, so the locals called them 'dragon trees'.

Dracaena marginata

MADAGASCAR DRAGON TREE

A name like the Madagascar dragon tree paints a pretty vivid picture, and the *Dracaena marginata*, a sculptural and dramatic plant with shiny, arching, sword-like leaves, makes a beautifully modern statement when displayed indoors.

CARE LEVEL
novice

LIGHT
bright, indirect +
full sun

WATER
low

SOIL
well-draining

HUMIDITY
low

PROPAGATION
stem cuttings

GROWTH HABIT
upright

POSITION
floor + covered
balcony

TOXICITY
toxic

Dracaena marginata is a tough, drought-tolerant plant with a robust root system that makes it an excellent houseplant. It thrives in bright light and while it will tolerate a lower-light position, you will generally find that growth is slowed and the plant produces smaller leaves with less intense colour. Some direct morning sun will be appreciated, but protect your plant from harsh afternoon rays.

When it comes to watering, less is definitely more. Always water deeply, but wait until the top half of the soil is dry before watering again. You'll find that you need to water less frequently in low-light situations. The development of brown leaf tips can mean that the plant isn't getting enough water or that it is receiving too much salt or fluoride. Because of this, the use of distilled water is advised.

The Madagascar dragon tree usually tops out at around 1.8 m (6 ft), which is still a very respectable size for an indoor tree. Thankfully, it doesn't mind being slightly pot bound, so repotting every two years should suffice.

Dracaena trifasciata 'moonshine'

Dracaena trifasciata

COMMON NAME SNAKE PLANT Syn: *Sansevieria trifasciata*

It may be a struggle to wrap your head around the fact that a number of *Sansevieria* species have recently been reclassified as members of the *Dracaena* genus. But as they say, a rose by any other name would smell as sweet, and this is certainly true of the *Dracaena trifasciata*.

CARE LEVEL
novice

LIGHT
bright, indirect

WATER
low

SOIL
coarse + sandy

HUMIDITY
low

PROPAGATION
division

GROWTH HABIT
rosette

POSITION
bookshelf or stand

TOXICITY
mildly toxic

While its Latin name may have changed, its common names remain the same. It is sometimes, unfavourably, known as mother-in-law's tongue, which references the sharp edges of its lovely upright leaves. We prefer the common name snake plant, and can assure you that this stylish succulent is one serpent you'll be more than happy to have hanging around the house.

Recognised in NASA's Clean Air Study for its incredible ability to remove four of the five toxins commonly found in our homes, *Dracaeana trifasciata* is more than just a pretty face. Add to that its ability to tolerate lower-light conditions and low water needs and you can see why the snake plant is such an enduring favourite among indoor gardeners.

Although this low-maintenance beauty needs little attention, be sure not to ignore it entirely. Good drainage is key and a potting mix specific to cacti and succulents will work well. Allow the soil to fully dry out between drinks, and always avoid the leaves when watering to prevent liquid pooling at the plant's centre, which can cause rot.

There are a number of lovely cultivars in a range of colours and patterning, but we have a particular soft spot for the delightful *Dracaeana trifasciata* 'moonshine' (pictured here), which features foliage in a dreamy silvery-green, but retains all the low-maintenance vibes synonymous with the plant.

It's worth noting that as this plant multiplies quickly, you may want to consider housing it in a plastic grow pot inside a cachepot, as their rhizomes have been known to break through fragile planters.

Plectranthus

Consisting of more than 350 fast-growing and low-maintenance species, this diverse genus can be found growing naturally in parts of Australia, Africa, India, Indonesia and the Pacific Islands.

Some species are edible, such as *Plectranthus amboinicus* (which tastes like a combination of oregano, thyme and mint), some are grown for their pretty foliage and flowers, such as *Plectranthus verticillatus* for its attractive, glossy green leaves and *Plectranthus neochilus* with its lavender-like blooms, while others still are grown for their medicinal properties.

CARE LEVEL
novice

LIGHT
bright, indirect

WATER
moderate

SOIL
well-draining

HUMIDITY
medium

PROPAGATION
stem cuttings

GROWTH HABIT
bookshelf or stand

POSITION
trailing

TOXICITY
toxic

Plectranthus australis

COMMON NAME SWEDISH IVY

Originally a popular houseplant in Sweden and with long, cascading stems reminiscent of ivy, it may be surprising to know that this super easy-care beauty is confusingly neither Swedish nor an ivy. It is, however, a fantastic indoor plant perfect for novice gardeners. Delightfully, this plant will thrive with very little maintenance and its incredible scalloped-edged, glossy foliage is a sight to behold, and even more so on the variegated cultivar pictured here.

In ideal conditions – bright, indirect light with access to some direct morning sun

– the Swedish ivy will grow rapidly. Good drainage is important, so use a well-draining potting mix and always allow the top 2–5 cm (¾–2 in) of soil to dry out between watering. The Swedish ivy's luscious foliage looks best cascading from a high position with the growing space it needs, so a spot on a shelf is ideal.

Be sure to keep it looking its best with a semi-regular grooming session – pinching the vine tips after flowering will prevent the plant from becoming leggy and can help you achieve a full shape.

Rhaphidophora cryptantha
A gloriously unique piece of foliage with a shingling growth habit that gives the *R. cryptantha* its common name of the shingle plant. It requires a solid totem on which to attach itself and grow upwards. Indoors, an iron bark or pressed coir totem provides the perfect support, without which the plant will remain very small and fail to thrive.

Rhaphidophora

Rhaphidophora is a genus in the family Araceae, consisting of approximately 100 species of vigorous, evergreen, climbing plants. They are naturally occurring in tropical Africa, stretching eastwards through Malesia and Australasia and on to the Western Pacific Region.

They are hemi-epiphytic, capable of beginning life as a seed in a tree and sending roots down to the soil, or starting in the ground and climbing upwards. In extremely rare cases, they are terrestrial rheophytes growing in fast-flowing water.

Rhaphidophora decursiva

COMMON NAME CREEPING PHILODENDRON

There has been much confusion over the two species *Rhaphidophora decursiva* and *Epipremnum pinnatum*, with almost all plants labelled as *E. pinnatum* in nurseries being in fact *R. decursiva*.

CARE LEVEL
novice

LIGHT
low–moderate

WATER
moderate

SOIL
well-draining

HUMIDITY
low

PROPAGATION
stem cuttings

GROWTH HABIT
climbing + trailing

POSITION
bookshelf or stand

TOXICITY
toxic

Perhaps their labels were switched in a tissue culture lab in Thailand, or when they first entered mass production. Either way, we can safely assure you that the plant you believed to be an *Epipremnum* is, in fact, a different genus entirely. To confuse matters further, this plant's common name is creeping philodendron as it was also once believed to be a philodendron.

Names aside, beginner gardeners can rejoice in the knowledge that they are the owners of a beautifully low-maintenance houseplant. While juvenile foliage is more elliptical (as exhibited in the specimen opposite), mature leaves become thick, leathery and pinnatifid, developing deep incisions. In some cases you may notice a stem extending without the appearance of leaves. This is an evolutionary technique the plant uses to search for a better position with more suitable growing conditions.

R. decursiva requires minimal care indoors and, like many aroids, makes a marvellous houseplant, either allowed to trail in a hanging planter or staked to climb by means of aerial roots. If you find growth slowing, your plant may be root bound and require repotting.

The creeping philodendron's water and light requirements are moderate. It is relatively drought hardy, but it will exhibit drooping and leaf curl if left too long between watering. Always allow the top 2–5 cm (¾–2 in) of soil to dry out prior to giving it another healthy drink, as it does not enjoy having wet feet. A position with bright, indirect light is favourable, but it will certainly tolerate a lower-light situation. This tough plant can also cope with cooler temperatures, happily growing outdoors year round in many climates.

Rhaphidophora tetrasperma

COMMON NAME **MINI MONSTERA**

One look at those petite, graphic leaves and you can see exactly why this guy is commonly referred to as the mini monstera. Other common names include the philodendron ginny or piccolo, but all are deceiving as although they are all members of the Araceae family, *Rhaphidophora tetrasperma* is neither a *Monstera* nor a *Philodendron*.

CARE LEVEL
novice

LIGHT
bright, indirect

WATER
moderate

SOIL
well-draining

HUMIDITY
medium

PROPAGATION
stem cuttings

GROWTH HABIT
climbing

POSITION
bookshelf or stand

TOXICITY
toxic

Hailing from Thailand and Malaysia, *Rhaphidophora tetrasperma* lives very happily indoors, providing all the graphic good looks and easy-going nature of its common moniker, but on a smaller scale. As it's a vigorous grower, particularly in the warmer months, you may find yourself needing to repot it yearly. It tends to do best with adequate support to climb – a moss pole, totem or trellis will do the trick. While it can be allowed to hang, it tends to result in leggy growth and reduced foliage size.

Water when the top 2–5 cm (¾–2 in) of potting mix is dry and avoid long periods of drought. Although the mini monstera may be forgiving of a little neglect, it will have a detrimental effect on growth. Standard household humidity won't bother *R. tetrasperma*, but it will certainly appreciate the added moisture from regular misting. It can be susceptible to root rot from over-watering, especially during the colder months, so be sure to facilitate adequate drainage year round and reduce watering during winter.

Schefflera

Schefflera is a large genus of flowering plants consisting of between 600 and 900 species. As such, it makes up around half of the plants in the Araliaceae or ginseng family. Named in honour of the 19th century Polish physician and botanist Johann Peter Ernst von Scheffler, the plants in this genus are a mix of trees, shrubs and woody vines, reaching heights of 4–20 metres (13–66 ft), with generally woody stems and palmately compound leaves. It is, of course, the umbrella-like shape of the foliage that inspires *Schefflera*'s common name, umbrella plant. The Australian umbrella plant (*Schefflera actinophylla*) and the dwarf umbrella plant (*Schefflera arboricola*; see opposite) are two of the most common *Schefflera* species enjoyed as houseplants.

CARE LEVEL
novice

LIGHT
bright, indirect

WATER
moderate

SOIL
well-draining

HUMIDITY
medium

PROPAGATION
stem cuttings

GROWTH HABIT
upright

POSITION
floor + tabletop

TOXICITY
toxic

Schefflera arboricola

COMMON NAME DWARF UMBRELLA PLANT

A tropical tree native to Taiwan and Hainan, as well as growing in many parts of Australia, the dwarf umbrella plant features the umbrella-shaped leaves for which the genus is renowned, but it is decidedly more compact than those of its full-size relative, *Schefflera actinophylla.*

Undoubtedly, the popularity of the dwarf umbrella tree is buoyed by its tolerance of neglect, but try not to take advantage of its forgiving nature. While it will tolerate a lower-light situation, it can lead to slowed, leggy growth. Bright, indirect light is your best bet for maintaining a lush, healthy specimen.

The dwarf umbrella plant is generally bushy, with an upright growth habit and plenty of shiny, leathery leaves. Smaller, juvenile plants work well on a tabletop or bench, while a floor spot is probably more suitable once the plant grows to maturity.

Schefflera can benefit from the occasional pruning to deal with stretched out growth or to tame an overgrown plant. Pruning a *Schefflera* is easy: simply cut off what is necessary to get it back to a size and shape you are happy with. You'll find that the plant rebounds quickly, looking fuller and lusher in no time.

A number of cultivars have been selected for variations in leaf colour and pattern. The cultivar *Schefflera arboricola* 'gold capella' (pictured), with its gold and green variegation, is a prize winner, having gained the Royal Horticultural Society's Award of Garden Merit.

Oxalis

Oxalis is a huge genus comprising more than 500 species. These successful plants have spread across the globe, with the majority of species found in tropical and subtropical South Africa, Mexico and Brazil. Although very sour to taste, some species are nonetheless cultivated for their edible leaves and tubers. Because of their ability to store energy in these tubers, some *Oxalis* have become noxious weeds that are quite resistant to weed control (so be conscious what you plant where), while a favoured few have become very popular plants in the garden and home.

With common names ranging from sourgrass and wood sorrel to false shamrock, many species look similar to clover and have various coloured pretty little flowers.

CARE LEVEL
novice

LIGHT
bright, indirect

WATER
moderate–high

SOIL
well-draining

HUMIDITY
medium

PROPAGATION
division

GROWTH HABIT
clumping

POSITION
tabletop

TOXICITY
toxic

Oxalis triangularis

COMMON NAME PURPLE SHAMROCK

The delightfully different *Oxalis triangularis* has deep purple or burgundy butterfly-wing or clover-shaped leaves, often with a lighter purple leaf centre. The leaves move delicately with the rhythm of the day and close like an umbrella at night. Only adding to their charm, they produce petite, pale purple to white bell-shaped flowers that sit gently above the foliage line.

Native to Brazil, Bolivia, Argentina and Paraguay, at full tilt this plant can reach heights and widths of 50 cm (20 in). It's a relatively low-maintenance beauty, but keep in mind that it can enter a dormant period if neglected or if temperatures get too high or low. If this happens, don't fret as this is a natural occurrence (some will go dormant every winter), and it doesn't mean your plant will die, but is instead entering a brief period of rest. Cut back the dead leaves, slow down on watering, so you don't drown the tubers that aren't using a tonne of energy, and keep out of overly bright light. Once you see new leaves begin to form, you can return it to its regular spot and watering schedule.

The pretty leaves of the *O. triangularis* can be used to decorate salads; just don't eat them in huge quantities or their acidity will upset your stomach. They are, however, toxic to pets when consumed in large enough quantities.

Tillandsia streptophylla

Tillandsia

With an incredible 650 species under its umbrella, the *Tillandsia* genus falls under the broader Bromeliaceae family. Growing in the wild in various environments from deserts and swamps to mountains and tropical forests in regions of the USA, Mexico, the Caribbean and Argentina, some species and cultivars are also well adapted to growth indoors.

What makes these plants rather unique is their ability to live seemingly on air alone, thus their common name 'air plants'. While they do sometimes produce small roots, they are only grown for structural support, as these plants absorb all of their nutrients and water needs via miniscule scale-like trichomes on the leaf surface.

With a huge array of structures, from the bulbous-looking *Tillandsia seleriana* to the spindly stems of the *Tillandsia pseudobaileyi* and the curly, light green leaves of the *Tillandsia streptophylla* (see opposite), this is an incredibly diverse genus. Their brightly coloured flowers and inflorescences range between vibrant pinks, blues, purples, yellows and reds.

Tillandsia usneoides

COMMON NAME **SPANISH MOSS**

Although resembling moss (hence its common name) and lichen, *Tillandsia usneoides* is actually an epiphytic flowering plant.

CARE LEVEL
novice

LIGHT
bright, indirect

WATER
moderate–high

SOIL
none

HUMIDITY
medium–high

PROPAGATION
offsets

GROWTH HABIT
trailing

POSITION
bookshelf or stand

TOXICITY
pet friendly

Resembling a tangle of hair, *Tillandsia usneoides* is generally made up of thin, light grey curled leaves that en masse can reach up to 6 metres (19½ ft) in length. Among the varieties and cultivars, there is a diverse range of leaf size, thickness and growth habit (such as the *Tillandsia usneoides* 'super straight').

Spanish moss enjoys lots of humidity, and as there is no potting mix to retain moisture it is important that you mist your plant almost daily, and give it a good soak roughly once a week. This schedule obviously depends on the climate of your home, the season and your particular specimen, but use it as a rough guide when figuring out your own care routine. To water your plant, it's best to submerge it in distilled water for 10 minutes. If it has a lot of leaves, make sure to gently swish them around in the water so they have a chance to absorb as much liquid as possible. It is very important to place the plant in a well-ventilated space once removed from water, as droplets left to sit on the leaves can cause your Spanish moss to rot. Although it's not a particularly hungry plant, you can occasionally spritz the leaves with a super-diluted bromeliad-specific liquid fertiliser if you feel it needs an extra boost.

At home, you can either gently fling your Spanish moss over existing plants, hang it from a hook, or display it tumbling out of a hanging vessel. Either way, just keep in mind that you will need to detach it easily for its regular bath.

Tillandsia xerographica

KING OR QUEEN AIR PLANT

One of the largest air plants available, this bad boy can grow to more than 90 cm (3 ft) wide and similarly tall when in flower.

CARE LEVEL
novice

LIGHT
bright, indirect–
full sun

WATER
low–moderate

SOIL
none

HUMIDITY
low

PROPAGATION
stem cuttings

GROWTH HABIT
rosette

POSITION
bookshelf or stand

TOXICITY
toxic

Its silvery grey-green leaves appear from a central rosette and slowly curl and taper off as they gently arch over the plant's central sphere. The flower, which can last for several months, appears on a tall, heavily branched inflorescence, with yellow, red, pink and purple tones. Native to dry, subtropical forests in Honduras, El Salvador, Guatemala and Mexico, where it grows in treetops or atop rocks, *Tillandsia xerographica* is, sadly, severely endangered.

Having evolved to survive in drier and brighter conditions, this air plant's large leaves require less water and more light than some other plants within the genus. This is true of most large- and grey-leaved *Tillandsia*, while those with smaller, greener leaves will generally have higher humidity and water requirements. For the king air plant, this means it should be watered roughly once a week in summer and monthly in winter, misting every few days. When your plant is ready for a drink, submerge it in distilled water for an hour or so before taking out and turning it upside down to allow any excess water to run off. It is vital that no water is left in the central 'vase' or your plant might rot. Staying moist for too long will also result in rot and likely plant death, so always place in a spot with lots of air circulation. You'll notice your plant turns more green when wet, before slowly returning to its normal grey tinge. Feed monthly after watering, by spraying with a super-diluted liquid fertiliser designed for bromeliads or air plants. These plants are slow growers, but will quickly become a hugely admired part of your indoor garden.

Spathiphyllum

Native to tropical parts of Southeast Asia and the Americas, this genus is probably most well known for its easy-care houseplants. The lush green leaves are complemented by a flower-like spathe, most commonly crisp white, but sometimes yellow or green.

These plants tick all the boxes for beginner gardeners and beyond. They're low maintenance, clean the air of toxins and can handle low-light conditions like a boss. We love the variegation of the *Spathiphyllum* sp. 'Picasso' and the dramatically broad leaves of the *Spathiphyllum* sp. 'Sensation'.

CARE LEVEL
novice

LIGHT
low–moderate +
bright, indirect

WATER
moderate

SOIL
well-draining

HUMIDITY
moderate

PROPAGATION
division

GROWTH HABIT
clumping

POSITION
tabletop + floor

TOXICITY
mildly toxic

Spathiphyllum sp.

COMMON NAME **PEACE LILY**

Peace lilies are a truly classic houseplant, making a regular appearance in indoor environments the world over where they are enjoyed for their lush glossy foliage. Perhaps some of their popularity also stems from the fact that they require very little maintenance. And, unlike a lot of indoor plants, the peace lily will happily flower profusely indoors, as long as it is doused in bright, indirect and gentle direct light. These blooms usually appear twice a year and will generally last for longer than a month. It is these white spathes, waving like peace flags, which perhaps give the plant its common name.

Peace lilies communicate dire thirst with drooping leaves. This is a sign that you have left it too long between drinks, so quickly get back to a regular watering schedule for the sake of your plant's health. If positioned in bright, indirect light, you will need to water your peace lily once the top 5 cm (2 in) of soil has dried out in summer (reducing to 6 cm/2½ in in winter), but if it's placed in lower light, wait until an extra 2 cm (¾ in) of soil has dried out before watering again.

Keep your plant tidy by dusting the leaves and pruning any spent flowers and leaves at the base of the stem. Mist your plant weekly, and fertilise fortnightly with a half-strength liquid fertiliser in the warmer months, upping to weekly when your plant starts flowering. Brown leaf tips are usually a sign of over- or under-watering. If they appear, monitor your plant's light and water conditions until you find a happier balance.

Zamioculcas

Part of the Araceae family, this genus has only one species: *Zamioculcas zamiifolia*. Commonly known as the Zanzibar gem or zz plant, it is native to eastern and southern Africa.

Over the years there have been false rumours that this plant is poisonous and can even cause cancer, but there is no evidence to back up these claims. On the contrary, there are a few studies that show the *Zamioculcas* is actually good for your health, effectively removing harmful chemicals, such as benzine, toluene, ethylbenzene and xylene, from the air.

CARE LEVEL
novice

LIGHT
low–moderate

WATER
low

SOIL
well-draining

HUMIDITY
low

PROPAGATION
division

GROWTH HABIT
clumping

POSITION
bookshelf or stand

TOXICITY
toxic

Zamioculcas zamiifolia

COMMON NAME **ZANZIBAR GEM**

Not only is the Zanzibar gem an effective air cleaner, it is also quite possibly the hardiest indoor plant going, so much so that it is sometimes referred to as the 'unkillable plant'. *Zamioculcas zamiifolia* has glossy, dark green, semi-succulent leaves with petioles that appear straight from the rhizomatous base of the plant and can grow up to 60 cm (2 ft) tall. If completely starved of water, the leaves will drop off and the plant will store its remaining water and energy in its stems until proper care is restored. That being said, we've seen these plants go unwatered for months and continue to look close to new. But try not to test your zz's hardiness, and implement a schedule where it is watered once the vast majority of potting mix has dried out.

Helpfully, the Zanzibar gem can also survive in rather low-light conditions, making it perfect for offices and darker rooms in your home. Its arching arms can be easily snapped off, so place your plant in a spot where people won't be regularly brushing past. It can be propagated by leaf cutting, but this is a slow-going process, so we recommend dividing your plant instead, which can be easily done by separating the potato-like rhizomes. The Zanzibar gem is relatively slow growing, so it doesn't need a lot of fertilising: once a month in summer, using a half-strength liquid fertiliser should do the trick.

Adiantum

This prolific genus of subtly beautiful and daintily delicate ferns has approximately 250 species within its ranks. The name *Adiantum* is derived from the Greek word *adiantos* meaning 'un-moistened', and refers to the fern fronds' ability to stay dry even underwater thanks to the finest layer of pubescence (hairs) covering their foliage. These bright green leaves sit on contrasting black stems and, amazingly, are self cleaning and actually repel water.

Hailing from far-flung regions of the world – from New Zealand and the Andes to China and North America – *Adiantum* grows terrestrially and epiphytically, and is famous for romantically sprouting around waterfalls.

Adiantum aethiopicum

COMMON NAME **COMMON MAIDENHAIR FERN**

As its common name suggests, this is probably the plant you think of when you hear the name maidenhair fern, with its delicate fronds and wiry black stems.

CARE LEVEL
green thumb

LIGHT
bright, indirect

WATER
moderate–high

SOIL
moisture-retaining

HUMIDITY
medium–high

PROPAGATION
division

GROWTH HABIT
clumping

POSITION
bookshelf or stand

TOXICITY
pet friendly

Adiantum aethiopicum is native to Africa, New Zealand and Australia, and it is one of only a small number of Australian natives that thrive indoors (joining the likes of the kentia palm, native river mint and staghorn fern). In the wild the maidenhair fern lives along creeks and in other moisture-rich environments, so you'll need to keep the soil moist at all times and water as soon as the surface of the potting mix has dried out; otherwise its leaves will crisp before your eyes. It enjoys moderate humidity but detests getting water directly on its foliage so avoid spritzing and opt instead for grouping it together with other plants. *A. aethiopicum* gets a bad rap for being very finicky and we've certainly had our battles in the past, but with the right care it can thrive and live a long, happy life. It's a fast grower with rhizomes that spread in creeping clumps, and elegantly arching light-green fronds that can reach 50 cm (20 in) in height. Pruning can keep your maidenhair fern tidy and prevent it from becoming too leggy. Cut off any dead foliage at the base of the stem with a sharp pair of secateurs. A good trim at the end of winter will also promote new growth come spring.

The maidenhair fern can be prone to scale so keep an eye out for any invading pests and act quickly to remove them. Thankfully, along with all true ferns, it is safe for pets.

Adiantum tenerum

COMMON NAME BRITTLE MAIDENHAIR FERN

A rare plant indeed, the brittle maidenhair fern or *Adiantum tenerum* is native to parts of North, Central and South America and the Caribbean, where it grows in shaded grottos and moist ledges.

CARE LEVEL
green thumb

LIGHT
bright, indirect

WATER
moderate–high

SOIL
moisture-retaining

HUMIDITY
high

PROPAGATION
division

GROWTH HABIT
clumping

POSITION
bookshelf or stand

TOXICITY
pet friendly

With a more ruffled leaf edge than the simpler common maidenhair fern, but retaining a similar fan-like shape, the new leaves of the brittle maidenhair will appear light green and slowly darken with age. For a touch of beautiful colour, opt for cultivar *Adiantum tenerum* 'gloriosum roseum'. Its pink-edged leaves, give it a distinctive look among a field of ferns.

These plants thrive in bright, indirect light, so keep them shielded from harsh, direct rays. They need a continuously moist potting mix, so water as soon as the surface of the soil dries out. Regular spritzing (with room-temperature water) will also help provide the high levels of humidity this maidenhair demands. Like a lot of ferns, the *Adiantum tenerum* is very sensitive to fertiliser, so always use a fertiliser that is specifically suited to delicate ferns and be sure to dilute it to half strength. Growth can slow substantially in winter, so stop fertilising until warmer weather returns and cut back on your watering schedule. At the beginning of spring, give your plant a good tidy up by snipping off dead foliage to make way for fresh growth.

Davallia

Native to Australia, Asia, Africa and the Pacific Islands, *Davallia* is made up of approximately 65 species that are very closely related to one another and often hard to distinguish between. It is the only genus within the Davalliaceae family.

Known for their aerial furry rhizomes and hairy stalks that resemble animal feet, these plants generally grow epiphytically, but they sometimes also occur lithophytically and terrestrially. The most commonly cultivated species within this genus are the *Davallia canariensis* (hare's-foot fern) and *Davallia fejeenis* (rabbit's foot fern; see opposite), which share the same pretty triangular-shaped fronds characteristic of these plants.

CARE LEVEL
green thumb

LIGHT
bright, indirect

WATER
moderate

SOIL
moisture-retaining

HUMIDITY
medium

PROPAGATION
division

GROWTH HABIT
clumping

POSITION
bookshelf or stand

TOXICITY
pet friendly

Davallia fejeenis

COMMON NAME **RABBIT'S FOOT FERN**

Native to Fiji, *D. fejeenis* has prominent furry, rabbit foot–like rhizomes that are synonymous with plants of this genus. Indoors, the rhizomes creep over the edge of their pot, and it is this unusual characteristic, along with their soft and airy lace-like fronds, for which the plant is favoured.

The rabbit's foot fern enjoys bright, indirect light, so ensure that it doesn't receive any harsh direct rays that will crisp its delicate foliage. Unlike most other ferns, the *Davallia* genus can tolerate slightly lower humidity levels, but you will still do best to keep the humidity at a moderate level. Remember that the rabbit foot's rhizomes are aerial, so don't bury them under soil when repotting.

Davallia fejeenis looks great in a hanging basket, where its rhizomes can grow all around the outside, or show it off on a high shelf. Although fairly resistant to infestation, white louse scale – a pesky fern pest – can develop as a result of minimal air circulation and soil dryness, going easily unnoticed and then multiplying rapidly. Aphids are also known to attack new unfurling fronds, particularly in spring, when they fly in through open windows. As with most ferns, it's important to avoid using any sort of leaf shine or harsh chemical insecticide on their sensitive fronds. Instead, opt for a gentle shower to remove dust and other nasties. In some cases a mild fern-specific insecticide can be used.

PTERIDACEAE family

Hemionitis

Hemionitis is a genus of ferns in the Pteridaceae family. Although it was first formally described by Carl Linnaeus in his 1753, *Species Plantarum*, the genus name predates him. It is derived from the greek word *hemionus* meaning 'mule', which references the belief that the plants were sterile.

  While there is some conjecture surrounding the genus, the Pteridophyte Phylogeny Group classification of 2016, suggests it is one of 20 genera in the subfamily Cheilanthoideae with only around five species.

CARE LEVEL
green thumb

LIGHT
bright, indirect

WATER
high

SOIL
moisture-retaining

HUMIDITY
high

PROPAGATION
division

GROWTH HABIT
clumping

POSITION
tabletop

TOXICITY
pet friendly

Hemionitis arifolia

COMMON NAME **HEART-LEAF FERN**

A particularly lovely species of miniature fern, aptly known as the heart-leaf fern for its heart-shaped leaves. Definitely one of the daintier members of the genus, this Southeast Asian native generally grows no taller than 20 cm (8 in). Its dwarf stature and moisture-loving habits make it ideal for use in terrariums, but it also makes a perfect potted plant, as long as the soil is kept consistently moist. Additionally, it can be mounted onto a piece of cork bark where it will happily grow epiphytically, requiring regular misting for hydration.

The heart-leaf fern's fuzzy black stems spray outwards, with the occasional high achiever reaching out above the rest. Its leaves first appear light green before darkening to a deep shiny green as they age. The leaves are also dimorphic, meaning that some are sterile and some are fertile.

The heart-leaf fern requires a moderate amount of attention, but with the right care it will reward you handsomely. Bright, indirect light and maintaining high humidity levels around the plant will go a long way to keeping this fern thriving.

Huperzia

There is some contention among botanists about the classification of this genus and the species that fall within it. Some split the genera into two (*Huperzia* and *Phlegmariurus),* while others believe the genus belongs to the Huperiaceae family. In this book we are referring to the genus as *Huperzia* from the Lycopodiaceae family.

Taxonomy aside, these plants, which are commonly referred to as firmosses, fir clubmosses or tassel ferns, have needle- or scale-like leaves. They are a fantastically adaptable genus, growing terrestrially, epiphytically and lithophytically in a huge variety of environments, from tropical to Arctic conditions and from sea level to alpine altitudes. Incredibly, they're one of the oldest living plant groups, predating ferns and most other Jurassic plants!

CARE LEVEL
novice

LIGHT
bright, indirect

WATER
moderate–high

SOIL
well-draining

HUMIDITY
high

PROPAGATION
division +
stem cuttings

GROWTH HABIT
trailing

POSITION
bookshelf or stand

TOXICITY
unknown

Huperzia squarrosa

COMMON NAME **ROCK TASSEL FERN**

Adored by plant lovers, this rare and beautiful fern ally, with graceful pendulus stems, is sadly endangered in the wild due to loss of habitat and over-harvesting. Its fuzzy, light green arms, which can reach 75 cm (2 ft, 3 in) long, dangle daintily downwards, dividing into further branches which are tipped by sporous tassels. Interestingly, this plant has medicinal properties and is sometimes used in the treatment of Alzheimer's and Parkinson's disease – a real miracle of nature.

Rock tassel ferns grow epiphytically or lithophytically, so a coarse, well-draining orchid-style potting mix filled with air pockets will enable healthy root growth. With small and shallow root systems, *H. squarrosa* doesn't like growing in too much media, and many growers place chunks of polystyrene in the pot before adding potting mix. It's also best not to repot it, as it often doesn't recover from the upheaval. Thankfully, it's absolutely fine to grow them in the same pot for years.

Its leaves will burn if placed in direct sunlight, so keep your plant in a bright spot, but shielded from harsh rays. In nature, rock tassel ferns grow near swamps and waterways, so be sure to mimic this moisture-giving environment by watering regularly. Fertilise sparingly, using quarter-strength fertiliser and one specifically suited to ferns and their allies, during the warmer growing seasons. This plant requires high humidity and good air circulation, so make sure it's sat on a pebble tray filled with water and that you regularly crack the windows.

specimen *Nephrolepis exaltata* var. *bostoniensis*

Nephrolepis

Commonly referred to as sword ferns for their long tapering fronds that stand erect or arch elegantly, *Nephrolepis* is a genus of about 30 species of fern, and the only one in the Nephrolepidaceae family. Growing terrestrially or epiphytically, these plants can be found in many tropical areas of Asia, Africa, Central America and the West Indies.

The plants' Latin name is derived from the Greek word *nephros*, meaning 'kidney', and *lepis*, meaning 'scale', which refers to the shape of the membrane that covers the sorus (a cluster of structures which produce and contain the spores), found on the undersides of the leaves. Due to the popularity of *Nephrolepis exaltata* var. *bostoniensis* – a 19th century variety first described in, you guessed it, Boston, Massachusetts – the whole genus is sometimes incorrectly referred to as Boston ferns. Whatever you choose to call them, these generally undemanding and resilient ferns make ideal houseplants.

Nephrolepis biserrata 'macho'

COMMON NAME MACHO FERN

Hardier and more robust than *Nephrolepis exaltata*, *Nephrolepis biserrata* is a Boston fern on steroids. Native to Florida, Mexico, the West Indies and Central and South America, this variety is commonly called the macho fern.

CARE LEVEL
novice

LIGHT
bright, indirect

WATER
moderate–high

SOIL
moisture-retaining

HUMIDITY
high

PROPAGATION
division

GROWTH HABIT
rosette

POSITION
bookshelf or stand

TOXICITY
pet friendly

Its broad, impressive fronds droop gracefully and can grow to over one metre (3 ft, 3 in) in length. It makes a particularly grand statement sitting on a plant stand or cascading from a hanging planter, with plenty of room to stretch out that fabulous foliage.

As with the Boston fern, keep the potting mix moist but not overly wet, and adjust your watering schedule according to the seasons (less will be required in winter). The thicker foliage of the macho fern tends to be more resilient than the Boston, making it slightly more forgiving of dry potting mix with less leaf drop and, therefore, less mess – win win!

While the *Nephrolepis biserrata* will happily live outside in a shaded spot, it can be invasive and get easily out of hand. Be conscious of your natural environment and plant only in containers, ensuring that it is unable to spread.

Nephrolepis exaltata var. bostoniensis

COMMON NAME **BOSTON FERN**

There's nothing quite like the spectacle of a bushy, mature Boston fern. It's an impressive plant that with the right care can bring incredible lushness to a space.

CARE LEVEL
green thumb

LIGHT
bright, indirect

WATER
moderate–high

SOIL
moisture-retaining

HUMIDITY
high

PROPAGATION
division

GROWTH HABIT
rosette

POSITION
bookshelf or stand

TOXICITY
pet friendly

For many, it is the fern that first springs to mind when talking about *Nephrolepis*, and it is an incredibly popular houseplant the world over. Relatively low maintenance, while care for the *Nephrolepis exaltata* isn't difficult, there are some important factors to get right, namely light and humidity. These plants love it steamy, so bi-weekly misting is advised and a position in a cool spot with indirect light is ideal. You can also sit the plant on a tray of pebbles filled with water for extra ambient moisture.

The soil should be kept consistently moist (but not soggy), allowing just the surface to dry out. Slightly less water is required in the cooler months when growth is slowed, but extended periods of dry soil will see the Boston's lush fronds crisp and die, which can be a messy predicament indeed. The good news is that these ferns are beautifully resilient and can bounce back from some neglect with a good prune and a return to consistent care.

Platycerium

This majestic genus consists of 19 species of plants, commonly known as elkhorn or staghorn ferns. Native to Australia, Africa, South America, Southeast Asia and New Guinea, they are largely tropical plants, but some species have also evolved to tolerate desert environments. You'll find them in almost every botanic garden, and their striking appearance is much admired by botanists and indoor gardeners alike.

The roots of mature plants in this genus grow in small dense clumps from a short rhizome that produces two types of fronds. The basal fronds are sterile, typically shield shaped and attach to the host tree on which the fern grows, covering the roots to protect them from damage. In some species, the tops of these fronds form an opening that catches falling debris and water on which the plant feeds. The fertile antler-shaped fronds extend outwards from the rhizome and bear spores on their undersides.

Platycerium bifurcatum

COMMON NAME ELKHORN FERN

Native to Australia, New Guinea and Java, this delightful epiphytic *Platycerium* looks equally beautiful as a huge wall-mounted specimen or a petite potted plant. In the wild it grows on tree trunks and can reach sizes up to 90 cm (3 ft) tall and almost as wide.

CARE LEVEL
novice

LIGHT
bright, indirect

WATER
moderate

SOIL
well-draining

HUMIDITY
medium–high

PROPAGATION
division

GROWTH HABIT
rosette + clumping + trailing

POSITION
bookshelf or stand

TOXICITY
pet friendly

With maturity, the plant is composed of a group of smaller plantlets, consisting of shield-like basal fronds that sit flush against the tree trunk from which thinner, forked, grey-green fertile fronds spring forth, resembling the antlers of an elk. These basal fronds turn brown as they age, but should never be removed. The fertile fronds, which usually average 25–90 cm (8–35 in) in length, are covered in fuzzy hairs that help protect the leaves from moisture loss and harmful sunrays.

Elkhorn ferns are often sold mounted to a piece of wood, but smaller specimens can also happily exist in a pot. In both cases, they like a humid environment and a regular watering schedule, only allowing the potting mix or moss to dry out just slightly in summer. Use a quarter-diluted liquid fertiliser in spring and summer only and keep your plant out of harsh direct sunlight.

Elkhorn ferns are fairly adaptable to the conditions in which they're grown. This extremely tolerant species can thrive in low humidity but will equally enjoy a more moist environment.

To mount your elkhorn fern, drill four screws into a wooden board (leaving them protruding somewhat from the board) before wrapping the elkhorn's roots in a ball of sphagnum moss. Place the moss ball on the wooden board and use fishing line to secure the plant in place, crossing back and forth along the moss and hooking the line over the various screws to secure it in place. Before long your elkhorn will have grown to cover the screws and fishing line.

Platycerium superbum

COMMON NAME STAGHORN FERN

Native to tropical and subtropical regions of Australia and parts of Indonesia and Malaysia, this impressively imposing fern shares many similar traits with its cousin the elkhorn fern.

CARE LEVEL
novice

LIGHT
bright, indirect

WATER
moderate

SOIL
moisture-retaining

HUMIDITY
medium–high

PROPAGATION
spores

GROWTH HABIT
rosette + clumping + trailing

POSITION
bookshelf or stand

TOXICITY
pet friendly

Like the elkhorn, it attaches itself to trees in the wild, sometimes also growing from rocks. It is also larger than the elkhorn – its basal fronds can grow up to one metre (3 ft, 3in) wide and the fertile fronds up to 2 metres (6 ft, 6 in) long. These fertile fronds, that splay out from the basal fronds like the antlers of a stag, are much broader than the elkhorn but they still fork into smaller branches towards the leaf end.

In the wild, the basal fronds at the top of the plant sit slightly out from the tree, allowing leaf litter, dead insects and water to collect in the fern nest, providing essential nutrients, such as potassium and calcium, for the plant. Although you may have read that feeding your staghorn fern tea leaves or banana peels is a good idea, especially indoors, such habits are not recommended. Rotting organic matter will invite insects, mold and sometimes fungus, as it takes far too long to break down in our home environments. It will, however, appreciate the occasional fern-friendly half-strength liquid fertiliser top-up in summer. These plants like a humid environment and lots of bright, largely indirect light (although they will happily lap up gentle morning rays). Be careful not to overwater your staghorn or the roots and basel fronds will rot.

Platycerium superbum generally comes mounted on a wooden board and is not easily propagated. Unlike the elkhorn fern, it is harder to divide so a lot of growers create new plants via spore germination. To do this, first sterilise a vessel (a pot or seedling tray will do) and enough coco coir to fill it, by pouring boiling water over both. The spores grow on the undersides of the fertile fronds and turn from green to a fuzzy brown once ripe. To collect the spores, wait until they ripen and then cut a few fronds off and place in a paper bag. Once the fronds dry out you can gently scrape the spores off with your fingers, evenly transferring them to your bed of coir. Do not bury the spores, but rather gently pat them down. It's advised to place a glass or plastic screen over your vessel to protect the spores, keep the area sterile and retain high humidity levels. Place your vessel in a warm spot with lots of bright, indirect light and be sure to keep the coir moist but the spores undisturbed by watering from the base into a saucer. In a matter of months (patience will be your friend!), baby staghorns will begin to appear and you can remove the glass or plastic covering, and transplant onto new wooden boards or into pots in about a year.

Howea

A tiny genus of just two palms, *Howea belmoreana* and *Howea forsteriana*, these plants are endemic to the magical paradise that is Lord Howe Island, off the east coast of Australia. First recorded in the late 1770s, the previously uninhabited island, although small, has a diverse range of environments and an incredible array of local and endemic flora and fauna. Along with other specimens, *Howea* palms were taken back to Europe by explorers and botanists, where they became the plant *du jour* of the 19th century.

Still popular today, the *Howea belmoreana* (commonly referred to as the sentry or belmore palm) has more arched fronds, with its crown resembling an umbrella, while the *Howea forsteriana* (kentia palm; see opposite) has a more upright habit. The sentry palm is more commonly found at higher elevations and is more tolerant of cooler temperatures, while the kentia is more abundant in the lower forests of the island.

CARE LEVEL
novice

LIGHT
bright, indirect

WATER
moderate

SOIL
well-draining

HUMIDITY
low–medium

PROPAGATION
seed

GROWTH HABIT
upright

POSITION
floor

TOXICITY
pet friendly

Howea forsteriana

COMMON NAME KENTIA PALM

Howea forsteriana, the more popular of the two *Howea* species, is an elegant, soft, dark green palm that grows rather happily indoors. While in the wild it can reach heights of 15 metres (50 ft), indoors it grows more slowly and will stay a manageable height.

These palms love rich, well-draining soil, so be sure to keep your plant well fed with a fortnightly liquid fertiliser in the warmer months. It enjoys a moderate amount of water, always allowing the top 5 cm (2 in) of potting mix to dry out between drinks. Like a lot of houseplants, kentia palms love to be placed outdoors when it rains. This will give them a good drink of clean water, help to flush their potting mix of any

salt build-up and clean the dust off their leaves. Just don't forget to bring your plant in before the sun starts to beat down on it and potentially burn the leaves.

Howea forsteriana can be prone to scale and mealybugs, so regularly give the leaves a quick checking over. If any unwanted visitors are present, give your plant a gentle hose down and spray and wipe with eco-oil. Check your leaves weekly and repeat if necessary until all pests are gone. Kentia palms are only propagated by seed; however, sometimes growers place more than one plant in a single pot. If you find that you do have two trunks, you can happily divide these into the two separate plants that they are.

Livistona

Livistona is a genus of fan palms from Asia, Australasia and parts of Africa, first described by botanist Robert Brown in Australia in the early 19th century. The name of the genus, however, pays tribute to the Baron of Livingstone, Patrick Murray, whose extensive plant collection formed the beginnings of the Royal Botanic Garden in Edinburgh. *Livistona* exists within the Arecaceae family and lists over 30 species, including the popular *Livistona australis* (cabbage tree palm) and *Livistona chinensis* (Chinese fan palm; see opposite).

CARE LEVEL
novice

LIGHT
bright, indirect +
full sun

WATER
moderate

SOIL
well-draining

HUMIDITY
low–medium

PROPAGATION
seed

GROWTH HABIT
upright

POSITION
floor

TOXICITY
pet friendly

Livistona chinensis

COMMON NAME CHINESE FAN PALM

With broad, green, fan-shaped fronds, *Livistonia chinensis* is a beautiful architectural palm. Native to China and Japan, outdoors it can grow to heights of 12 metres (40 ft), with mature leaves that are lobed and droop attractively towards the ground. Indoors, with the correct care, these palms can reach 3 metres (10 ft), so place your plant somewhere it can make a tropical statement.

A relatively low-maintenance plant, the Chinese fan palm does need a few hours of direct sun every day, with lots of bright, indirect light for the remaining daylight hours. It is a slow grower, but this can be helped along with a monthly application of fertiliser during the warmer seasons. It enjoys a moderate amount of water, allowing the top 5 cm (2 in) of potting mix to dry out before watering again. Be careful not to over-water your palm as it can cause root rot and lower the general well-being of your plant, making it more susceptible to pests. Dusting the leaves and spritzing them to keep humidity levels up will act as a pest deterrent.

Brown leaf tips are generally a sign that your palm isn't receiving enough water. Palms are commonly purchased as large plants that have been growing in their pots for a number of years to get them up to size, by which time their potting mix has become depleted of nutrients. As a result, it is not uncommon for their soil to become hydrophobic. You can combat this by applying an organic soil wetting agent or repotting with fresh potting mix.

Rhapis

Commonly referred to as lady palms, *Rhapis*, consisting of about 10 species, are native to Southeast Asia where they have been cultivated for many centuries. The genus name, *Rhapis*, is derived from the Greek word for needle, referring either to the narrow foliage or sharp, pointed tips.

A type of fan palm, *Rhapis* are generally on the shorter side relative to other palm genera, making them perfect houseplants. The tallest of the genus, *Rhapis humilis* (slender lady palm) reaches heights of about 5 metres (16 ft) outdoors, while the more common *Rhapis excelsa* (lady palm; see opposite) only manages 4 metres (13 ft). Their fronds are all similarly palmate in nature, with the *Rhapis subtilis* having particularly slender and elegant leaves. Along with the listed species, there are some interesting and harder-to-get-your-hands-on cultivars including a stripy white or yellow variegated variety of *Rhapis excelsa*.

CARE LEVEL
novice

LIGHT
bright, indirect

WATER
moderate

SOIL
well-draining

HUMIDITY
low

PROPAGATION
division

GROWTH HABIT
upright

POSITION
floor

TOXICITY
pet friendly

Rhapis excelsa

COMMON NAME LADY PALM

The most commonly grown *Rhapis* is the hardy *Rhapis excelsa* or lady palm. Its dainty green fronds grow from multiple fibrous sheaths, appearing like fireworks excitedly bursting forth. Because of its clumping, nature, it can grow as wide as it does high when planted outdoors. It is generally more expensive to purchase than other palms due to its slow-growing nature, but don't let this put you off as it is incredibly hardy and will eventually get to a good size without too much effort on your behalf.

These palms thrive in bright, indirect light but will also happily tolerate lower-light conditions. Just keep clear of harsh direct sun which will burn the leaves. It isn't terribly fussy about humidity, but keep away from heaters and give it the occasional spritz if the air feels dry. Lady palms enjoy a moderate amount of water, allowing the top 5 cm (2 in) to dry out between drinks. Never allow the potting mix to dry out entirely, as this will cause the fronds to brown. Like most palms, *Rhapis excelsa* is not overly hungry, but if you notice the leaves getting a yellow tinge it will benefit from a top-up of fresh potting mix or a dose of half-strength liquid fertiliser. Keep your palm tidy by pruning off brown fronds, and if you find that new growth is appearing half dead, this might mean that there is a fungal issue and you are best to sacrifice the stem from which it came to stop it spreading.

Lepidozamia

This genus, endemic to Australia, consists of just two species: *Lepidozamia hopei* and *Lepidozamia peroffskyana* (see opposite). Part of the broader Zamiaceae family, these plants are cycads that tend to look a little like ferns or palms.

Naturally occuring in wet rainforests in New South Wales and Queensland, *Lepidozamia* have been cultivated for both garden and home. Junior specimens, more suited to a life indoors, make highly sculptural additions to plant collections.

CARE LEVEL
novice

LIGHT
bright, indirect

WATER
low

SOIL
coarse + sandy

HUMIDITY
low

PROPAGATION
seed

GROWTH HABIT
clumping

POSITION
tabletop

TOXICITY
toxic

Lepidozamia peroffskyana

COMMON NAME **SCALY ZAMIA**

With dark green, glossy arched leaves that emerge from a scaly brown trunk, scaly zamia looks very similar to a palm tree once fully mature. It is one of the tallest species of cycads in the wild, reaching heights of 7 metres (23 ft). Its male or female seed cone appears from the centre of a rosette about 50 cm (20 in) high, rising to one metre (3 ft, 3 in) when it slowly spirals up to release pollen. Junior specimens without trunks (and thus no cones) are more suited to the size constraints of a life indoors. Note that the seed has toxic attributes, but this is unlikely to be a concern with indoor specimens that are kept small and immature.

In the wild, *Lepidozamia peroffskyana* usually grows in sandy soils. Indoors, it is tolerant of dry spells and generally doesn't require fertiliser, but it's best to water before the potting mix fully dries out. Place in a spot with lots of bright, indirect light, and keep an eye out for scale, cleaning them off and spraying and wiping with eco-oil at the first signs. Although slow growers, with the right conditions these plants will thrive for many years, allowing you to enjoy their impressive, almost prehistoric vibe.

Drosera

With nearly 200 species, *Drosera* is one of the largest genera of carnivorous plants. Found all over the world, bar Antarctica, they are an incredibly resilient group of plants that thrive in nutrient-poor environments by sourcing their food from insects instead. Their common name, sundew, refers to the dew-like mucilage found along the leaves of the plants, which acts as both an attractor and trap for prey.

  These plants generally have a rosette growth habit, but those rosettes can be anywhere from 1 cm (½ in) to one metre (3 ft, 3 in) tall, with equally diverse looks. From the pink spoon-like leaves of *Drosera falconeri*, to the thin lacy leaves of *Drosera capensis* and the sea creature-esque *Drosera ordensis*, this is a hugely curious genus that you will definitely enjoy getting to know. Charles Darwin certainly did, writing in a letter: 'I care more about Drosera than the origin of all the species'.

CARE LEVEL
expert

LIGHT
bright, indirect +
full sun

WATER
high

SOIL
moisture-retaining

HUMIDITY
medium

PROPAGATION
leaf cuttings +
division

GROWTH HABIT
rosette

POSITION
windowsill

TOXICITY
mildly toxic

Drosera sp.

COMMON NAME **SUNDEW**

These interesting creatures have tentacle-like leaves that secrete a sweet mucilage to attract prey. It is this same sticky substance that also ensnares them. Some tentacles will move to further trap the prey or quickly catapult them to the centre of the plant, and within about 15 minutes the insect will have died from exhaustion or by drowning in the mucilage. The plant then secretes enzymes that dissolve the insect and allow its nutrients to be absorbed. *Drosera* sp. have flowers that sit high above the plant to avoid potential pollinators becoming trapped before they're able to do their important job.

Most sundews require full sun, while a few are happy in bright, indirect light. If growing your plant outdoors, keep it in a protected spot away from wind and overly harsh direct light. Always water with distilled water and be sure to keep the soil constantly moist. You can sit your pot in a saucer filled with water to ensure that the potting mix never dries out.

If kept outdoors, your plant will happily catch its own prey, but indoors you will need to feed it a small insect, such as a wingless fruit fly, a few times a month. Never fertilise your sundew, as it gets all the nutrients it needs from its prey and it may damage the plant's weak root system. You can propagate most *Drosera* sp. by division or by taking a leaf cutting with a small section of stem still attached and floating it in distilled water until little plantlets appear in a matter of weeks.

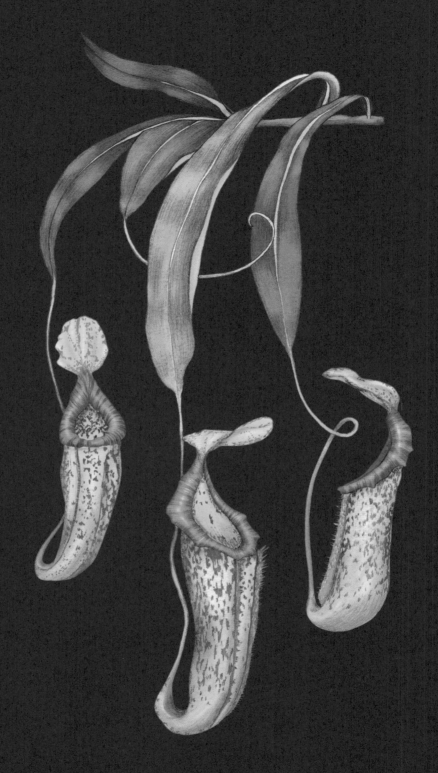

specimen *Nepenthes sibuyanensis* × *talangensis* (× red dragon)

Nepenthes

The sole genus within the Nepenthaceae family, *Nepenthes* are identified by the unusual pitchers that grow from their leaf tips. They have a shallow root system and most are terrestrial, but a small number are epiphytic or lithophytic. Generally, the thin winding stems of these plants clamber their way up trees in the wild, but a small number of species cling to the ground.

The pitchers, which are round or tube shaped or somewhere in between, are often quite phallic in appearance. Plants usually produce two types of pitchers. Large pitchers sit at the base of the plant and even larger ones, which first often wrap their stems around branches to help support the plant, appear closer to the top. Insects and arachnids (and sometimes even larger creatures like rats) are attracted to the pitcher's colour, nectar and scent. This has proven a successful recipe for humans, too, as people tend to become seriously obsessed with these plants. The prey fly or fall into the pitcher and are then trapped by the strategically placed hairs, waxy internal sides and sticky liquids. The plants then digest nutrients from their prey.

Nepenthes sp.

COMMON NAME PITCHER PLANTS

There are more than 170 curious and wonderful species (and even more hybrids, both naturally occurring and cultivated) of pitcher plants. As such, identification of individual plants is often very hard, even for horticulturalists.

CARE LEVEL
expert

LIGHT
bright, indirect +
full sun

WATER
high

SOIL
well-draining

HUMIDITY
high

PROPAGATION
stem cuttings

GROWTH HABIT
climbing

POSITION
covered balcony

TOXICITY
mildly toxic

These plants grow in many different regions of the world, with most species found in Borneo, Sumatra and the Philippines, and in smaller numbers in Australia, China, India, Indonesia, Sri Lanka, Malaysia, Madagascar, the Seychelles and New Caledonia. Some species are only known to occur in very limited areas, such as *Nepenthes deaniana*, which is only found on the summit of Thumb Peak in the Philippines, while other species, like *Nepenthes mirabilis*, grow in many countries.

Nepenthes can be broadly grouped into two types of plants: highland and lowland. Lowland plants live in hot and humid environments, while highland species require warm days and cold nights to thrive. These plants mostly all enjoy humid but well-ventilated conditions, and should be kept clear of extreme temperatures and draughts. They much prefer rain or distilled water rather than tap water, and never use chemical fertilisers or leaf

shines. Their soil should stay relatively moist, but well-draining and, generally speaking, they like bright conditions with a good amount of gentle direct sunlight in order to produce pitchers. *Nepenthes* can be propagated by seed or stem cuttings. Cuttings should be rooted in sterilised and damp coir, and kept in a closed humid environment (under glass or similar). They should root after one to two months and begin to form pitchers after six months.

Pitcher plants are not necessarily for beginner gardeners, but a few of the easier-care species include *N. maxima*, *N. sibuyanensis* and *N. ventricosa*. These plants were of great interest to early explorers and botanists, and continue to be revered and collected around the world.

As with all plants, they should never be removed from their natural environment, rather purchased from a reputable nursery.

*Nepenthes sibuyanensis ×
talangensis (× red dragon)*

Nepenthes sp.

Darlingtonia

This carnivorous genus holds only one species in its ranks, the *Darlingtonia californica*, or cobra lily. Native to Northern California and Southern Oregon, this pitcher plant is similar to species within the *Heliamphora* and *Sarracenia* genera, which are also part of the Sarraceniaceae family. Differentiating it, though, is its unusual shape, which resembles that of a cobra snake rearing its head, forked tongue and all. Like all pitcher plants, it uses waxy surfaces and strategically placed hairs to trap its prey, with the addition of fake and hidden exits which disorients the insect prey.

Despite being considered both a low and highland plant, the cobra lily only grows in specific habitats, where cool water can be found flowing underneath or nearby. It's worth noting that wild populations of *Darlingtonia* have not been assessed since June 2000, so it is difficult to say what numbers look like in its natural environment.

CARE LEVEL
expert

LIGHT
bright, indirect +
full sun

WATER
high

SOIL
moisture-retaining

HUMIDITY
low

PROPAGATION
division +
stem cuttings

GROWTH HABIT
clumping

POSITION
covered balcony

TOXICITY
pet friendly

Darlingtonia californica

COMMON NAME **COBRA LILY**

Although a pretty tricky plant to grow, the sheer beauty of this species makes it worthy of inclusion. The pitcher is coloured light green, red or a mottled mix of the two, while its 'tongue' secretes an intoxicating nectar that lures prey. Its pretty flowers, which tower over the pitcher, attract pollinating insects that hopefully do their job before becoming prey themselves.

One of the most important care factors for this plant is to keep the roots cool and moist in order to emulate its natural environment. Water regularly with distilled water, making sure the soil stays moist at all times by placing the pot in a tray filled with water. On hot days, you can place ice cubes on top of the soil to keep the roots cool. It will also require cool overnight temperatures.

Darlingtonia californica does best in bright, indirect and direct light as long as it's not too hot. As it is accustomed to growing in nutrient-poor bogs, you won't need to fertilise your plant, but it will need access to insects to feed off. If it's inside, pop open a window to encourage insects to appear.

Your cobra lily will likely pause growth during winter, as it requires these cooler temperatures in order to thrive in the warmer months. Towards the end of this dormant period you can propagate your plant (if it's big enough) by dividing any clumps or taking a cutting of the stolon that has baby plants attached and some roots. Place this cutting in sterilised coco coir in a super-humid environment and watered regularly with cool water.

Dionaea

Charles Darwin famously wrote that *Dionaea muscipula* is 'one of the most wonderful (plants) in the world'. We couldn't agree more. Darwin was speaking of the single species within the *Dionaea* genus, which belongs to the Droseraceae family. Joining it are the closely related *Drosera* (sundews; see page 286) and *Aldrovanda* (the waterwheel plant) in this family of carnivorous plants.

The *Dionaea* genus joins an unusual group of plants that move in response to stimuli. Other such plants include the *Mimosa pudica* (the sensitive plant) whose leaves gently close if touched or if movement is sensed, and the *Cornus canadensis* (creeping dogwood), which opens its petals and shoots out pollen at incredible speeds. In the case of *Dionaea,* insects trigger hairs lining the inner sides of its traps, which then snap shut and allow the plant to digest its prey.

CARE LEVEL
expert

LIGHT
full sun

WATER
high

SOIL
well-draining

HUMIDITY
high

PROPAGATION
division + leaf cuttings

GROWTH HABIT
rosette

POSITION
covered balcony

TOXICITY
pet friendly

Dionaea muscipula

COMMON NAME VENUS FLY TRAP

One of the most readily available carnivorous plants in nurseries, the venus fly trap only grows naturally in very small areas of North and South Carolina in the USA. Sadly, due to human activity, it is nearing extinction in the wild, where it grows in nutrient-poor bogs and has evolved to feed on insects and arachnids to survive.

These petite plants don't usually grow more than 10 cm (4 in) high, although their delicate white flowers often tower above the leaves and traps. The traps appear at the end of some, but not all, stems and are coloured lime green or red. Little hairs on the inside of the traps alert the plant to the presence of prey, and if one hair is tapped twice in quick succession or two hairs are tapped within 20 seconds, the trap is triggered to swiftly close. Larger eyelash-like hairs lining the edge of the trap help to enclose the prey. Once the prey is digested, the trap opens back up again, ready for business. Traps only have two to three trapping motions up their sleeve before they die off, so be careful not to touch them, even if you really, desperately want to, as it could eventually cause the whole plant to die off. These are slow-growing plants that like lots of sun and continually moist potting mix. Despite the threat they pose to insects, they are happily non-toxic to cats and dogs.

Sarracenia

These captivating carnivorous plants generally have long, thin, trumpet-like tubes topped with an open lid, which provides them with their common name, trumpet pitchers. They also produce delicate upside-down, umbrella-like flowers that appear in spring. There are about 10 species within the genus, all of which are native to the USA and Canada. Unfortunately, these plants are under serious threat from habitat destruction and the plant and cut-flower industry. While only a small number of species are known, there are many hybrids, both naturally occurring and cultivated, making particular plants hard to identify.

These carnivorous beauties attract prey with their bright colours, patterns and sweet-smelling nectar. Unsuspecting victims slip on the edge of the trumpet rim, falling into the viscous liquid below. They become quickly trapped by the liquid, waxy walls and downward-pointing hairs, before being slowly digested.

CARE LEVEL
expert

LIGHT
full sun

WATER
high

SOIL
moisture-retaining

HUMIDITY
medium

PROPAGATION
division

GROWTH HABIT
clumping

POSITION
covered balcony

TOXICITY
pet friendly

Sarracenia sp.

COMMON NAME **TRUMPET PITCHERS**

From the albino-looking *Sarracenia leuco-phylla* to the more bulbous red *S. rosea* and the horizontal pitchers of the *S. psittacina*, there are many beautiful species of *Sarracenia* to explore, and an even greater number of cultivars and hybrids. These plants aren't one of the easiest plants to grow, so don't be disheartened if you don't get it right the first time round.

Sarracenia need at least five to six hours of direct sunlight a day, followed by or preceding lots of bright, indirect light. The less sun, the less vibrant the patterns on your plant and, more importantly, the less healthy your plant will be. A spot on a balcony is great, or a very sunny windowsill. Outdoors, these plants can trap their own prey, but inside a monthly feed of insects during the warmer seasons will keep your

plant topped up with the nutrients it needs. These plants love water, albeit rain or distilled and not tap. Always water from below by placing a saucer or bowl beneath your planter and ensuring the water comes half way up your pot. This will also provide ambient humidity for your plant. In winter ditch the water, just ensure sure the potting mix still remains moist at all times.

Trumpet pitchers love warm environments, but need three to four months of cooler weather over winter, where they enter dormancy and get some much needed beauty sleep. Towards the end of winter, it's useful to prune back leaves, pitchers and flowers, to allow the sun to reach fresh growth as it appears in spring. Like all carnivorous plants, they like nutrient-poor soil that's heavy on the coco coir.

CACTI +
SUCCULENTS

Cereus

Native to South America, this genus has over 30 columnar cacti within its ranks, from the 10 metre (33 ft) tall and shrubby *Cereus repandus* (Peruvian apple cactus; see page 306) to the slightly smaller knobbly *Cereus hildmannianus* 'monstrose' (monstrose apple cactus). They are noteworthy for the beauty of their fleeting night-blooming flowers, which appear in late spring. Their fruit, which is edible in some species, is round to ovular and brightly coloured, popping against the greens and greys of *Cereus* stems.

Cereus cacti bloom at night in sync with their nocturnal pollinators, such as moths and bats, and also in an effort to conserve water loss, as blooming requires a lot of energy. Other cacti that employ this method include *Selenicereus grandiflorus*, a trailing plant that produces glorious burnt orange or crisp white flowers.

Cereus hildmannianus 'monstrose'

COMMON NAME MONSTROSE APPLE CACTUS

With undulating, twisting, sculptural stems, this species of *Cereus* stands out within its genus.

CARE LEVEL
novice

LIGHT
full sun

WATER
low–moderate

SOIL
coarse + sandy

HUMIDITY
none

PROPAGATION
stem cuttings

GROWTH HABIT
upright

POSITION
tabletop

TOXICITY
pet friendly

Commonly known as the monstrose apple cactus, it can reach heights of 7 metres (23 ft) outdoors, but indoor varieties are usually smaller specimens. As such, it is generally only the mature outdoor plants that bloom – their stunning white flowers (often with a pinkish hue) awaken overnight and, if you're lucky, stay open into the morning, too. Attracting pollinating hummingbirds, bats and insects in their native Brazil, these blooms eventually turn into a pink-red fruit that is said to taste similar to dragon fruit.

This cacti needs lots of direct sunlight and a low to moderate amount of water. It can be propagated by stem cuttings; just be sure to allow the ends to callus before replanting. Because of its spikes, keep this plant in a spot where you won't chance brushing past it. Equally, be careful when repotting or propagating and always wear thick gloves and handle with care.

Cereus repandus

COMMON NAME PERUVIAN APPLE CACTUS

Those that say size doesn't matter haven't met *Cereus repandus*. Considered a weed in its native South America where it grows in abundance, this tall, ribbed, columnar plant is appreciated by cactus lovers the world over. As such, it is the most widely cultivated *Cereus* species and it makes for a striking ornamental plant.

CARE LEVEL
novice

LIGHT
full sun

WATER
low–moderate

SOIL
coarse + sandy

HUMIDITY
none

PROPAGATION
stem cuttings

GROWTH HABIT
upright

POSITION
floor

TOXICITY
pet friendly

Thanks to its erect growing habit and impressive height, the Peruvian apple cactus is often used in gardens to create a living fence. Its thick stems can grow to 10 metres (33 ft) in an outdoor environment, but thankfully much less indoors. Still, this prolific grower is best contained in a sturdy pot that will support the cactus as it reaches its lofty extent.

In addition to striking stems, *Cereus repandus* has some culinary significance. As its common name suggests, the plant produces a red fruit known as Peruvian apple, which has a delicious white flesh.

Caring for the Peruvian apple cactus, as is the case with many cacti, is decidedly low key. The biggest non-negotiable for this desert dweller is sun and plenty of it. Without adequate light, growth will become slow and etiolated and you may find your cactus getting its lean on as it searches for light. During its active growth period, water deeply once the coarse and sandy potting mix is completely dry, but wait much longer between drinks as the weather cools.

Curio rowleyanus

Curio

A newly described genus of flowering plants in the Daisy family, *Curio* consists of approximately 20 species that were previously classified as *Senecio*. Aptly named after the Latin word for curious, they certainly are a quirky collection of succulents. Particularly popular as houseplants are the small group of scrambling trailers referred to fondly as the 'string of' posse, including the delicate string of pearls and the wacky string of dolphins, among others. With the right care they all grow happily indoors, bringing just the right amount of weirdness to a plant gang.

These distant cousins of the common dandelion hail from the hot, dry regions of South Africa, where their interestingly shaped leaves have adapted perfectly to the harsh conditions. While the succulent banana-like leaves of *Curio radicans* look the most 'typical' in their morphology, the pea-shaped beads of the *Curio rowleyanus* are far more unusual and probably the most effective at handling drought. It is when these plants reach maturity and begin producing generous blooms of pleasantly scented flowers that their position within the Daisy family becomes more obvious.

Curio radicans

COMMON NAME STRING OF BEANS Syn: *Senecio radicans*

Less finicky than its fellow 'string of' pals, *Curio radicans* is a lovely trailing succulent that thrives in both arid and tropical environments in its native South Africa. It loves warm climes and grows quickly during spring and summer.

CARE LEVEL
novice

LIGHT
bright, indirect

WATER
low

SOIL
coarse + sandy

HUMIDITY
none

PROPAGATION
stem cuttings

GROWTH HABIT
trailing

POSITION
bookshelf or stand

TOXICITY
toxic

C. radicans has plump, succulent, curved leaves reminiscent of beans, bananas or fish hooks (inspiring its many common names) that grow around 2.5 cm (1 in) long. These leaves are attached to long tendrils that cascade attractively over the pot's edge, adding a tonne of texture to any indoor garden. It looks great on a shelf or in a hanging planter, and the small white flowers, which appear throughout the year, will reward your senses with a strong cinnamon scent.

Once established, the string of beans is semi-drought tolerant, so you'll do best to water once most of the potting mix has dried out. Wrinkling stems and leaves are a sign of serious thirst, so be sure to give your plant a drink before it shows such signs of stress.

The string of beans is easy to propagate. If your plant starts to look a little bald on top or if you're after a bushier specimen, a stem cutting can be popped back into the soil to thicken up the plant. Stems can also be wrapped back on top of the pot for the same effect.

Fertilise monthly during the warmer seasons, holding off once the weather cools. Its shallow root system means regular repotting is not required; just ensure the pot is heavy enough to balance the weight of the long stems.

Curio rowleyanus 'variegata'

Curio rowleyanus

COMMON NAME **STRING OF PEARLS** Syn: *Senecio rowleyanus*

Native to southwest Africa, *Curio rowleyanus* is a curious succulent that grows between rocks and other plants that provide protection from the intense arid conditions of the region. In the wild, the stems stretch out until they find the ground and then root, forming dense mats.

CARE LEVEL
green thumb

LIGHT
bright, indirect

WATER
low

SOIL
coarse + sandy

HUMIDITY
low

PROPAGATION
stem cuttings

GROWTH HABIT
trailing

POSITION
bookshelf or stand

TOXICITY
toxic

Indoors, the string of pearls is grown for its unusual foliage: masses of long, beaded tendrils that look incredible cascading over the edge of a pot in a beautifully bright position. Its delicate appearance belies the fact that the string of pearls is a vigorous grower that can quickly reach lengths of around 90 cm (3 ft) in the right growing conditions.

The string of pearls' leaves allow the plant to maximise water storage while minimising the amount of surface exposed to the harsh sun, thereby conserving water. As with other *Curio* species, these leaves feature a translucent 'window', an adaptation that allows sunlight to illuminate the leaf interior so the plant can maintain high levels of photosynthesis without overheating in its hot native habitat.

Curio rowleyanus needs access to bright light with at least a few hours of direct sunlight a day, preferably in the morning. If the stems become straggly and their beads small and stunted, simply remove them, giving the plant a solid haircut. You can pop healthy stem tip cuttings back into the pot to thicken up growth, creating a full, lush plant. During summer you can expect to see clusters of white daisy-like flowers that are small but fragrant.

Curio talinoides var. *mandraliscae*

COMMON NAME BLUE CHALK STICKS

Another South African native, this stylish succulent appreciates sun, warmth and a well-draining potting mix. Although generally unfussy when grown outdoors, as with other blue-grey succulents, it can be slightly temperamental indoors, its unhappiness usually stemming from inadequate access to light.

CARE LEVEL
green thumb

LIGHT
full sun

WATER
low

SOIL
coarse + sandy

HUMIDITY
none

PROPAGATION
stem cuttings

GROWTH HABIT
clumping

POSITION
windowsill

TOXICITY
toxic

Blue chalk sticks can certainly be grown indoors, as long as its position is bright with access to direct sunlight for much of the day. Alternatively, it works beautifully in a container outdoors or used as ground cover in drought-tolerant gardens.

Differing from its trailing relatives, blue chalk sticks is a dwarf shrub with a clumping growth habit that produces upright pencil-like foliage in an incredible shade of silvery-blue. It is generally slow growing, reaching heights of only around 30 cm (12 in), so pruning is not usually an issue, but you can pinch it back to keep it at a certain height or to promote branching.

Blue chalk sticks should be kept on the dry side, so only water once the potting mix has completely dried out. Like all succulents and cacti, it doesn't require much fertiliser – simply feed with a half-strength liquid fertiliser three or four times during the whole growing season.

Winterocereus

Within the Borzicactus tribe, *Winterocereus* is one of a number of genera of mainly columnar cacti with distinctive blooms that feature a double perianth (the parts of the flower that surround a plant's sexual organs). Originating in Bolivia, Peru and Argentina, *Winterocereus* are pollinated by birds rather than insects.

Some sources claim that *Winterocereus aurespinus* (see opposite) is the sole species (which is perhaps why there is so little information available about the genus, but this is hard to verify). The golden rat tail cactus, as it is commonly known, was previously classified in the *Cleistocactus* genus, the etymology of which comes from the Greek word *cleistos* meaning 'closed', and refers to the flowers produced by these plants that never completely open.

There has been much movement in and out of the *Cleistocactus* genus, which will no doubt continue as more research and molecular DNA sequencing is carried out.

CARE LEVEL
novice

LIGHT
bright, indirect–
full sun

WATER
low

SOIL
coarse + sandy

HUMIDITY
low

PROPAGATION
stem cuttings

GROWTH HABIT
clumping

POSITION
bookshelf or stand

TOXICITY
pet friendly

Winterocereus aurespinus

COMMON NAME GOLDEN RAT TAIL Syn: *Cleistocactus winteri*

Commonly known as the golden rat tail, this is one quirky cactus. The long narrow stems of *Winterocereus aurespinus* (which can grow up to one metre/3 ft, 3 in) arch and drape from a tightly clumped base, reminiscent of Medusa's head adorned with snakes. Those stems are covered in short, bristly, golden spines, and with the addition of vivid orange-pink blooms, it makes for a sculptural and unique addition to any indoor plant collection. Unlike most other cacti, the golden rat tail trails beautifully from a shelf with its golden, textured stems reaching towards the floor.

Despite its exotic appearance *W. aurespinus* is easy to cultivate and, therefore, perfect for novice gardeners. It needs lots of bright light and while it will enjoy some direct sun, direct afternoon rays should be avoided. Water regularly in spring and summer, but ensure its coarse potting mix is fully dry before watering again and cut back significantly during the winter months. As with most cacti kept indoors, scales and mealybugs can make a happy home on the golden rat tail, sneakily hiding among the spines. This is mainly due to the lack of extreme temperatures and conditions that they would normally experience outdoors, so keep a close eye out for the little devils on a regular basis.

specimen *Aloe vera*

Aloe

This delightfully dramatic and highly prolific genus contains more than 500 species. Native to parts of Africa, Arabia, Jordan and some smaller islands in the Indian Ocean, most *Aloe* consist of succulent rosettes of fleshy leaves that grow straight from the ground, with a smaller number of species growing trunks. Their spiky flowers bloom high above the leaves in bright oranges, reds and yellows.

While most people are familiar with the soothing medicinal benefits of *Aloe vera*, other species, such as the stunningly spiralled *Aloe polyphylla* (see page 323), the spiky-edged *Aloe perfoliata* and steely grey *Aloe hereroensis,* are grown for their ornamental value.

Aloe × 'Christmas carol'

COMMON NAME **CHRISTMAS CAROL ALOE**

Green leaves spotted with raised red markings and a star-like form give this hybrid aloe a particularly festive cheer.

CARE LEVEL
novice

LIGHT
bright, indirect–
full sun

WATER
low

SOIL
coarse + sandy

HUMIDITY
low

PROPAGATION
offsets

GROWTH HABIT
rosette

POSITION
windowsill

TOXICITY
mildly toxic

The pinky-red flowers that usually appear in autumn only add to the colourful pop of this plant. It makes a great indoor aloe as it is slow growing and stays rather small, reaching just 30 cm (12 in) wide and tall.

The Christmas carol aloe has low water requirements and can be pretty drought tolerant once mature. Water deeply, ensuring that the water escapes out the drainage hole at the base of the pot, and then allow the potting mix to fully dry before watering again. It does require direct sunlight, so place on a windowsill or balcony, ensuring that you bring it indoors during the winter months if you are likely to experience frost.

This plant can be propagated via the tiny offsets it produces. Like all succulents, you will need to allow the offset (or cutting in the case of other succulents) to dry out for a few days before replanting to lessen the chance of bacterial infection.

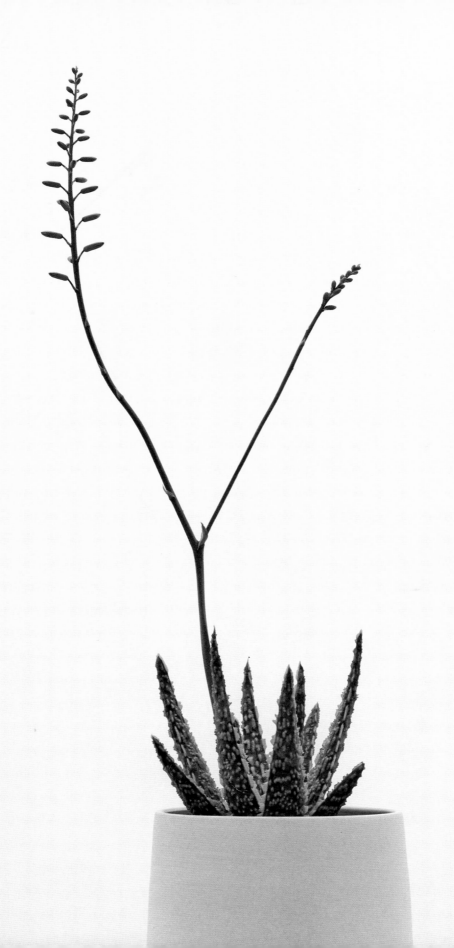

Aloe polyphylla

COMMON NAME **SPIRAL ALOE**

This seriously dramatic *Aloe* is endemic to Lesotho, the tiny kingdom within South Africa, where it is considered a threatened species. Its juicy, succulent leaves spiral out beautifully from a central rosette once the plant reaches maturity.

CARE LEVEL
novice

LIGHT
bright, indirect–
full sun

WATER
moderate

SOIL
coarse + sandy

HUMIDITY
none

PROPAGATION
seed

GROWTH HABIT
rosette

POSITION
tabletop

TOXICITY
toxic

Grey-green in colour, the leaves have a serrated edge and a spiky brown tip. Being stemless, this is a compact plant, but it makes a great statement indoors with its bold geometry. Keep in mind that it requires a little extra work than some of its peers, but if you're lucky enough to get your hands on one, you'll want to treat it right.

Unusually for a succulent, the spiral aloe has moderate water needs, which evolved as the plant adapted to growing on cooler, wetter mountainsides where it also learned to tolerate a little frost and snow. When watering, try to aim for the potting mix rather than the centre of the plant, to ensure that water doesn't get trapped among the leaves. In addition, when potting your plant, angle the *Aloe polyphylla* slightly so it's not facing straight up. This will help to prevent water getting stuck in the top of the plant and has the added bonus of allowing you to get a better view of that wonderful spiral.

Fertilise with a half-strength liquid fertiliser in the growing seasons, and keep your plant tidy by cutting off old leaves at the base. Always be careful whenever you handle your spiral plant as its spikes can do you an injury.

Crassula 'Buddha's temple'
This quirky hybrid was created in the 1950s by American botanist and director of the Huntington Botanical Gardens in California, Myron Kimnach. It is truly a work of art with its tightly stacked, slightly folded leaves creating a square column topped with a large sphere of colourful flowers – a veritable feast of geometric shapes.

Crassula

This large genus of around 300 species contains a huge diversity of plants, varying extensively in size, leaf colour, texture and shape. Belonging to the same family as the genera *Sedum* (see page 386) and *Kalanchoe* (see page 371), *Crassula* are native to Africa, Australia, New Zealand, Europe and the Americas. The genus name is derived from the Latin *crassus*, which means 'thick', and refers to the leaves that have evolved to store water and tolerate harsh environments.

While some plants within the genus have a more 'traditional succulent' look, such as the hugely popular *C. ovata* (see page 326), there are also many unusual, almost alien-like, species and hybrids that will make your heart flutter. There's the tightly overlapping leaves of the *C.* 'Buddha's temple' that form a stunning square columnar rosette, from the top of which a mass of flowers bursts forth; or the cutely rounded cup-like leaves of the *C. umbella* and the *C. umbella* 'Morgan's beauty', which looks like overlapping grey pebbles dotted with bright pink clumps of flowers.

Crassula ovata

JADE PLANT

The jade plant, or *Crassula ovata*, is a fleshy, low-maintenance succulent that is said to bring good luck and financial prosperity to those that care for them. This makes it a popular plant to gift, especially among certain Asian cultures.

CARE LEVEL
novice

LIGHT
bright, indirect +
full sun

WATER
low

SOIL
coarse + sandy

HUMIDITY
none

PROPAGATION
stem cuttings

GROWTH HABIT
upright

POSITION
floor

TOXICITY
mildly toxic

Originating in Mozambique and South Africa, this plant has evolved to tolerate semi drought–like conditions, which is a useful trait for forgetful plant parents.

Indoors, the small, shiny and ovular succulent leaves are more likely to be a darker jade, while outdoors in brighter environments, they are often lighter in tone with red-tinged edges. Starting out compact, the jade plant will eventually achieve dwarf tree-like proportions in maturity, and if you treat it right, sweet little bursts of light pink or white flowers will appear in spring.

Direct morning and indirect afternoon sunlight is best, and a low quantity of water will suffice. Always err on the side of under-watering your *Crassula ovata*, and adjust according to how much sun and heat your plant receives at any given time. A feed with a quarter-strength succulent fertiliser once a month during the growing seasons will be useful, but isn't totally essential as this isn't a super-hungry plant. There are lots of cultivars of the *Crassula ovata*, so once you've mastered the original, you can move on and try the others.

Crassula perforata

STRING OF BUTTONS

Native to South Africa, this attractive succulent has sharp, petite, stacked leaves that grow two at a time opposite one another, spiralling around a rope-like stem to create a mosaic feel.

CARE LEVEL
novice

LIGHT
bright, indirect

WATER
low–moderate

SOIL
coarse + sandy

HUMIDITY
none

PROPAGATION
stem + leaf cuttings

GROWTH HABIT
clumping + trailing

POSITION
bookshelf or stand

TOXICITY
pet friendly

The grey-green leaves often have red tips and the plant produces pale yellow or white flowers in spring when grown in brighter conditions. The string of buttons can grow to 60 cm (2 ft) tall and 90 cm (3 ft) wide. Initially upright in habit, once the stems get close to maturity, the weight of the leaves encourages the plant to sprawl beautifully over the edge of its pot.

Indoors, you'll want to give your string of buttons lots of direct morning light and indirect afternoon light, otherwise it can get leggy and lethargic. Keep an eye out for both symptoms and move into a sunnier spot if needs be. Although the

Crassula perforata is drought tolerant, you are best to water deeply once most of the potting mix has dried out.

The string of button's leaves can be brittle, so be careful when handling, but keep in mind that they can be propagated by stem as well as leaf cuttings, so any breakages can be simply reinserted into the pot (after the standard callusing period). Happily, *C. perforata* is virtually pest resistant, so you're unlikely to have to battle with creepy crawlies. Fertilise in spring with a succulent solution diluted to half strength and this should keep your plant going year round.

Bowiea

We're suckers for little weirdos, and when it comes to kooky plants the *Bowiea* genus does not disappoint. With only one species identified, *Bowiea volubilis* is a bulbous perennial that shoots up delicate stems, which cling to anything they can find. What makes these plants unusual is their light green or paper brown onion-like bulbs that sit largely above the soil surface.

Native to eastern and southern regions of Africa, *Bowiea volubilis* can withstand quite harsh conditions, while adding a definite flair to your plant collection.

Bowiea volubilis

COMMON NAME **CLIMBING ONION**

While the climbing onion does not have a particularly appealing common name, its unusual aesthetic makes it a rather special specimen. The dainty green stems of *Bowiea volubilis* slowly weave and wander until they find something to cling to. If you don't want them falling in a tangled mess around the bulb (no judgement if this is your preferred style!), it's best to train them up a trellis of whatever shape you prefer. Small star-like light green flowers will appear in spring.

A much-loved feature of this plant is its large visible bulb, which stores water and makes it tolerant of a little neglect. Although you want to be careful not to over-water your plant as the bulb could rot, be sure that you don't let all the potting mix dry out between drinks. The climbing onion likes bright, indirect and gentle direct light, and it isn't a fan of high humidity. It's also not a particularly hungry plant, but it may benefit from a cactus-friendly fertiliser once a month or so when you can see it's growing.

Your climbing onion may enter a dormant period where the stems die off, but there are mixed reports about when this usually happens, with some growers never experiencing a die back at all. If it does happen, simply prune off any dead stems, water a lot less frequently and wait patiently until new stems appear. This might happen almost immediately or you may have to wait until the season changes.

specimen *Ceropegia ampliata*

Ceropegia

There is no shortage of common names among the *Ceropegia* genus, from the parasol flower to the bushman's pipe, many of which reference the glorious flowers the plants produce. The Latin name for the genus, however, was decided by none other than Carl Linnaeus himself, who described it in his Species Plantarum volume 1, published in 1753. Believing the flowers to be reminiscent of wax fountains, the scientific name for the genus was derived from the Latin words *keros* (wax) and *pege* (fountain).

This diverse group of plants contains around 180 species native to much of Southern Asia, Sub-Saharan Africa and Australia, but this number is steadily growing as more species are identified. *Ceropegia* share strong similarities with stapeliads and plants within the *Brachystelma* genus, both of which are members of the Apocynaceae family. There is some contention that many other species should be moved into the *Ceropegia* genus, a decision that would increase the number of species to more than 750. What is less contentious, however, is that many *Ceropegia* make beautiful houseplants, providing delicacy to an indoor jungle.

Ceropegia ampliata

Inspired by their striking blooms, *Ceropegia ampliata*'s common names (including horny wonder and condom plant) are enough to make many a plant lover blush.

CARE LEVEL
green thumb

LIGHT
full sun

WATER
low

SOIL
sandy + coarse

HUMIDITY
medium

PROPAGATION
stem cuttings

GROWTH HABIT
climbing + trailing

POSITION
bookshelf or stand

TOXICITY
toxic

This distinctive beauty is certainly not your run-of-the-mill houseplant and it is one of the most interesting plants you are likely to come across. Its succulent, leafless rambling stems produce inflated balloon-like flowers of white and yellow pinstripes that are topped with emerald green cages.

In addition to its unique appearance, the condom plant has a distinct method of pollination. The inside of the plant's tubular flowers are lined with hairs that temporarily trap insects. While captured within the flower, pollen sacs become attached to the unsuspecting prisoners who are released after a number of days as the flower deteriorates. Pollination then takes place once the insects clamber into another flower. Nature is truly wonderful.

A hanging basket or plant stand is perhaps the most effective way to display this showstopping plant indoors, allowing its network of twining stems to cascade. The condom plant needs at least four hours of direct sunlight a day and will withstand a fair amount of drought. Water deeply, soaking its coarse potting mix, then wait until the soil has completely dried out before watering again. During the cooler seasons, only water just enough to keep the stems from shrivelling.

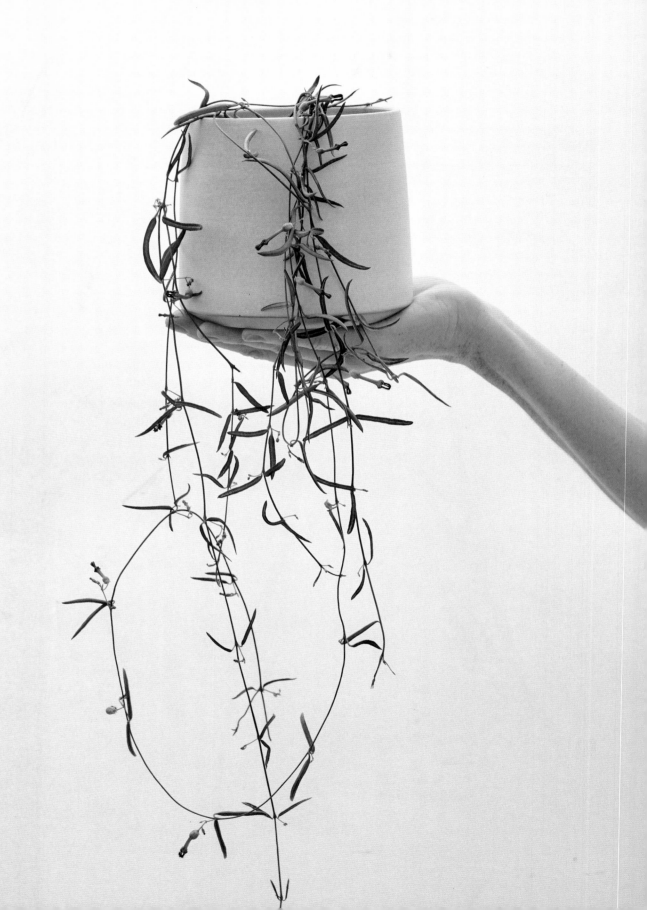

Ceropegia linearis

COMMON NAME **STRING OF NEEDLES**

Living up to its common name, the string of needles, with its intricate and delicate vines adorned with a multitude of slender, fleshy leaves, brings beautiful elegance to an indoor jungle.

CARE LEVEL
novice

LIGHT
bright, indirect

WATER
moderate

SOIL
well-draining

HUMIDITY
medium

PROPAGATION
stem cuttings

GROWTH HABIT
trailing

POSITION
bookshelf or stand

TOXICITY
pet friendly

Ceropegia linearis grows from tuberous rootstock, reaching up to 2 metres (6 ft, 6 in) or more in length. While in the wild it scrambles over the ground or twines into surrounding vegetation for support, indoors it looks incredible trailing down a bookshelf or plant stand.

Its flowers, similar in appearance to those of its close relative the chain of hearts, are another beautiful feature of this plant, which only add to its charm and good looks. To encourage blooms and general plant health, the string of needles likes plenty of bright light and will enjoy a few hours of direct morning sun. It is far more tolerant of dry soil than wet, so pot in a well-draining mix and allow the majority of soil to dry out between drinks.

Be mindful when repotting *C. linearis* and only increase its pot size in small increments, to avoid having excess soil that can result in the roots becoming waterlogged. Smaller plants can be upsized to encourage growth, but mature specimens will continue to thrive in their pots for several years without the need for repotting.

Ceropegia woodii

COMMON NAME CHAIN OF HEARTS

With dainty, heart-shaped succulent leaves growing along fine chains, the pretty *Ceropegia woodii* is a delicate and textural beauty.

CARE LEVEL
novice

LIGHT
bright, indirect

WATER
moderate

SOIL
well-draining

HUMIDITY
medium

PROPAGATION
stem cuttings

GROWTH HABIT
trailing

POSITION
bookshelf or stand

TOXICITY
pet friendly

Ceropegia woodii's deep green leaves are patterned with silver, and in the case of the variegated chain of hearts, they are also mottled with shades of pink and cream. In addition to its special foliage, in the right conditions it will produce purple tubular blooms that are cute as a button.

Indoors, the long vines of this South African native can reach 60–120 cm (2–4 ft) and, as such, this plant looks stunning trailing from a hanging vessel or perched atop a shelf. It is not suitable for low-light environments, so place your chain of hearts where it will receive plenty of bright, indirect light and some direct morning sun if possible. Over-watering

can be a death sentence for this succulent vine, so allow its potting mix to thoroughly dry out between drinks.

The chain of hearts produces small, bead-like tubers at intervals along its vine giving it the appearance of rosary beads, its other common moniker. These bulbs can be planted like seeds to grow new plants or replanted in their original pot to thicken up the mother plant.

Fun fact: hummingbirds are attracted to the flowers of the chain of hearts, so if you're living in the Americas, hang your plant in a sheltered spot outdoors during the summer months to attract some feathered friends.

Disocactus

Often confused with the similarly named but visually disparate *Discocactus* genus, *Disocactus* may sound like less of a party but it is in fact a lot more fun. Made up of only a handful of species, *Disocactus* grow epiphytically and lithophytically in their native tropical Mexico, Central and South America and the Caribbean.

While there is some flux over the species identified within the genus, two current members, which also helpfully exhibit the forms *Disocactus* take, include *Disocactus ackermannii*, with its flat, trailing, leaf-like stems and bright red blooms, and *Disocactus flagelliformis* (see opposite), which is cylindrical with spiky stems and shockingly bright pink flowers.

CARE LEVEL
novice

LIGHT
bright, indirect–full sun

WATER
low–moderate

SOIL
coarse + sandy

HUMIDITY
none

PROPAGATION
stem cuttings

GROWTH HABIT
trailing

POSITION
bookshelf or stand

TOXICITY
toxic

Disocactus flagelliformis

COMMON NAME RAT TAIL CACTUS Syn: *Aporocactus flagelliformis*

Formally known as *Aporocactus flagelliformis*, this impressive trailing cactus can grow up to 1.2 metres (3 ft, 9 in) in length. Native to Mexico, it is the most popular species within the *Disocactus* genus. It can be identified by its green stems and small brown spiky spines. In mid to late spring, a multitude of bright pink blooms appear, covering a large portion of the plant.

The rat tail cactus is grown indoors and out, but inside your plant will need lots of bright, indirect and gentle direct light to thrive. It will appreciate a good amount of water in spring and summer, allowing only half the potting mix to dry out before watering again, but back right off in autumn and winter and let the potting mix dry completely before giving it another drink.

This sculptural, pendant plant looks incredible displayed in a hanging pot or tumbling down a shelf; however, a weighty pot is recommended to ensure that it doesn't overbalance after a growth spurt. Repot your rat tail cactus every couple of years into a slightly larger planter to help balance its growth.

Echeveria

A classic and easily identifiable genus of succulents, *Echeveria* are native to Mexico and Central and South America. Their compact rosettes of leaves look like a gently opening rose and vary hugely in colour, from pale grey (*Echeveria lilacina*) and deep red (*Echeveria agavoides*), to green (*Echeveria* × 'abalone') and almost black (*Echeveria affinis* 'black prince').

Named after the 18th century Mexican botanical artist and naturalist Atanasio Echeverría y Godoy, *Echeveria* have long been cultivated. Containing about 150 species, there is also a plethora of hybrids and cultivars to explore.

Echeveria laui

COMMON NAME LAUI

Native to Mexico, this ghostly white-blue fleshy succulent may be slow growing, but once mature it will produce delightful little orange-pink blooms atop towering stems that stretch above the central rosette.

CARE LEVEL
green thumb

LIGHT
bright, indirect

WATER
low

SOIL
coarse + sandy

HUMIDITY
none

PROPAGATION
leaf + stem cuttings/
offsets

GROWTH HABIT
rosette

POSITION
tabletop +
windowsill

TOXICITY
pet friendly

Reaching only about 15 cm (6 in) in diameter, it will stay petite and make a great indoor plant companion if you're lucky enough to get your hands on one.

These plants only need a small amount of water. Soak through the soil, then wait until the potting mix has completely dried out before watering again. Don't water from overhead; instead, try and water directly onto the potting mix to avoid the potential of water pooling on the leaves and causing them to rot. With that in mind, it's also essential that *Echeveria laui*

has good air circulation, so don't pack it in too closely next to other plants, and crack a window every now and then. Be sure to remove any dead leaves, so they aren't given the opportunity to rot.

Like most *Echeveria*, the laui can be propagated by stem or leaf cutting, or by separating the offsets from the mother plant. Whichever option you take, always allow the cutting to callus over for a few days before planting it. Despite the desire to stroke this pretty plant, try not to as fingers will leave unsightly marks.

Echeveria × 'Monroe'

COMMON NAME MONROE

A hybrid of unknown parentage, *Echeveria* × 'Monroe' is a compact rosette of succulent pointy leaves that are green in lower-light conditions, but turn a steely grey with rosy ends when given more sun. It has a lovely dusty look, so try not to touch your plant too much as it will rub off this attractive feature.

CARE LEVEL
novice

LIGHT
bright, indirect

WATER
low–moderate

SOIL
coarse + sandy

HUMIDITY
none

PROPAGATION
stem cuttings/offsets

GROWTH HABIT
rosette

POSITION
tabletop +
windowsill

TOXICITY
pet friendly

Monroe requires lots of bright, indirect light and some gentle direct morning rays to thrive. Make sure you shuffle your plant into an adequately bright spot during the darker winter months. If it's not getting enough light, your plant will begin to look leggy and lose its compact, round shape. To remedy this, you can cut the head off the plant and repot it back into the potting mix, ensuring that it then goes into a sunnier position. In winter, or if under stress or just due to the natural cycle of life, your plant might shed its lower leaves. Be sure to tidy these off by cutting or removing them from the potting mix so they don't rot and attract fungal issues.

Echeveria × 'Monroe' has low to moderate water needs during summer, which you should further reduce in winter. Always water directly into the potting mix, ensuring that the water doesn't collect in the centre of the rosette where it can encourage rot in the plant.

Cotyledon

The *Cotyledon* genus is part of the Crassulaceae family and consists of around 10 shrubby succulent species, along with many more cultivars and hybrids. With generally small leaves, they come in a diverse range of shapes and textures, from furry to powdery-looking, round to pointed. All have tubular flowers with curved edges that sit well above the leaf line and grow in shades of red, orange and pink.

We love the wiggly grey leaves of the *Cotyledon undulata* (silver ruffles), the peachy bundles of bell-shaped flowers on the *Cotyledon orbiculata* (pig's ear) and the cute furry paws of the *Cotyledon tomentosa* (bear's paw; see opposite).

CARE LEVEL
novice

LIGHT
bright, indirect

WATER
low–moderate

SOIL
well-draining

HUMIDITY
none

PROPAGATION
stem cuttings

GROWTH HABIT
upright

POSITION
tabletop

TOXICITY
mildly toxic

Cotyledon tomentosa

COMMON NAME **BEAR'S PAW**

This sweet little succulent has small furry leaves with dark red tips (or teeth) that resemble a baby bear's paws and claws. There is also a variegated cultivar with delightful creamy streaks on its leaves. The bear's paw is a densely branched plant that maxes out at around 50 cm (20 in).

Native to South Africa, it is a relatively common indoor succulent and for good reason – it's easy to care for and cute to boot. It needs lots of bright, indirect light and deep watering once most of the potting mix has dried out. The succulent leaves are great at storing water, so always err on the side of under- rather than over-watering, making sure that you water even less frequently in winter when your plant will go into a semi-dormant state. Overly

moist soil can cause root rot, fungal diseases and leaf drop.

Orange-pink tubular blooms should appear in early spring, adding lovely colour to your indoor jungle. This is also a good time to commence fertilising, with a half-strength succulent-friendly fertiliser every month while the weather is warm.

We recommend propagating your bear's paw via stem cutting instead of the more challenging leaf cutting. You'll need to wait until your plant is mature, so the stems are long enough to cut from, but once it reaches size, take a cutting with a few leaves attached and allow the end to callus over for a few days before inserting into well-draining, coarse potting mix. Roots should start to grow in a few weeks.

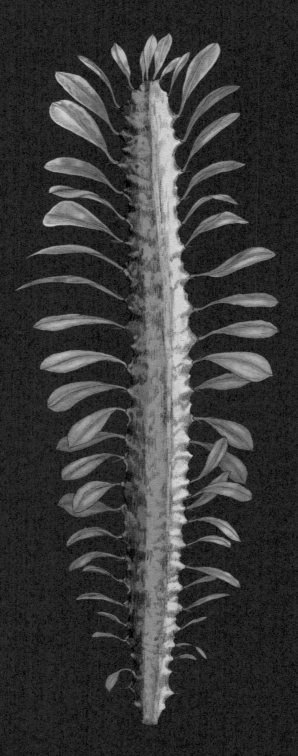

specimen *Euphorbia trigona*

Euphorbia

This prolific and hugely diverse genus with an astonishing 2000 listed members can be found all over the world. Varieties include leafy species, such as *Euphorbia pulcherrima* (poinsettia), the cactus-like *Euphorbia trigona* (African milk tree), the more classic-looking succulent *Euphorbia myrsinites* (myrtle spurge), and the strange spherical blob of *Euphorbia obesa* (baseball plant).

Native to regions in Africa and Madagascar, some species of *Euphorbia* are commonly confused with cacti. Unlike cacti, however, their flowers are simple and they have thorns rather than spines that are equally as sharp. Another major difference is that *Euphorbia* produce a highly poisonous, milky sap, which is considered an extreme irritant. Avoid getting it in your eyes at all costs, as it has been known to cause temporary and even permanent blindness. With this in mind, it's probably best not to keep these plants at all if you have pets or small children. When repotting, propagating or repositioning, always wear gloves and to be extra safe throw on a pair of shades, too.

Euphorbia ingens

COMMON NAME **CANDELABRA TREE**

Native to Southern Africa, this tree-like succulent can reach heights of 12 metres (39 ft). With a thick trunk and rounded crown that resembles an orb held at the top of the plant, it's a striking shape, which attracts birds looking to nest.

CARE LEVEL
novice

LIGHT
bright, indirect +
full sun

WATER
low

SOIL
coarse + sandy

HUMIDITY
none

PROPAGATION
stem cuttings

GROWTH HABIT
upright

POSITION
floor

TOXICITY
toxic

Younger plants that are kept indoors will often grow as a single branch, which generally suits smaller spaces. *E. ingens* blooms from autumn to winter, with an abundant mass of yellow-green flowers.

Coming from dry areas and savannahs, the candelabra tree doesn't like a lot of water, and it can usually survive some periods of drought. During the plant's growing seasons, it's best to allow the majority of the soil to dry out before watering again, and allow all of it to dry out in winter. *Euphorbia ingens* loves warmth, so make sure you bring any plants indoors in the cooler months. Always ensure that your plant gets a few hours of direct sun, or loads of bright, indirect light. Fertilise once every few weeks during spring and summer with a succulent-appropriate fertiliser.

As with all *Euphorbia*, the sap of the candelabra tree is highly toxic so exercise caution when handling your plant. It is worth noting that many larger candelabra-type euphorbia are sold in peat moss, some with pebbles glued on top of the potting medium, which becomes rather precarious, particularly when growing this plant indoors. We recommend opting for alternative specimens if this is the case at your local plant store.

Euphorbia tirucalli

COMMON NAME **FIRESTICKS**

Native to East Africa, India and the Arabian Peninsula, this succulent tree has bright green, long, pencil-thin stems that branch as it grows.

CARE LEVEL
novice

LIGHT
bright, indirect–
full sun

WATER
low

SOIL
coarse + sandy

HUMIDITY
none

PROPAGATION
stem cuttings

GROWTH HABIT
upright

POSITION
tabletop

TOXICITY
toxic

When exposed to direct sunlight, these stems turn a series of beautiful sunset shades from yellow to red, giving them their common name 'firesticks'. Inconspicuous leaves usually drop off as the plant matures, which is when it also starts producing tiny yellow flowers.

In the wild, *Euphorbia tirucalli* grow into large trees up to 7 metres (23 ft) high, but indoors the smaller cuttings from which the plants grow look more like a bundle of pencils, which begin to resemble sea coral once they change colour. To encourage this signature orange colouring, make sure your firesticks has access to mostly direct light. It has low water requirements, be careful to never over-water your plant. Fertilise once a month during the warmer seasons and you'll be rewarded with lots of lovely growth.

While firesticks make a striking plant, as with all *Euphorbia* species, it is severely toxic. Always handle with extreme care (wear glasses and gloves) and perhaps opt for another genus if you have pets or children. Despite its toxicity, sadly scale and mealybugs will happily feast on *Euphorbia*, particularly when kept indoors.

Euphorbia trigona

AFRICAN MILK THISTLE

Native to West Africa, this green and sometimes red-tinged upright clumping succulent is often mistaken for a cactus, and understandably so. Its branched clumps grow up to 2 metres (6 ft, 6 in) tall and 50 cm (20 in) wide, while its three- or four-sided stalks are lined with thorns that are almost hidden by small leaves that shoot from the same spot.

CARE LEVEL
novice

LIGHT
bright, indirect + full sun

WATER
low–moderate

SOIL
coarse + sandy

HUMIDITY
none

PROPAGATION
stem cuttings

GROWTH HABIT
upright + clumping

POSITION
covered balcony

TOXICITY
toxic

A slow-growing succulent, the African milk thistle is relatively fuss free. It does, however, require about four hours of direct sunlight a day and lots of bright, indirect light either side. It likes a little more water than your average succulent, and it will need a drink once the top 5 cm (2 in) of potting mix has dried out. During seasonal changes or when preparing for a growth spurt, its leaves can yellow and drop off, while at other times this can be a sign of over-watering. Dry, brown leaves, on the other hand, can indicate inadequate watering.

Propagate your *Euphorbia trigona* via stem cutting, allowing the end to callus for a few days, then dip in rooting hormone before planting out. When cut, the African milk thistle will secrete a sticky milky sap that can cause extreme skin irritation, so it is essential to wear protective gear when handling this plant. This will not only protect you from the sap but the sharp thorns, too.

Gasteria

Native to South Africa, these compact plants, with their chubby, rough leaves, are commonly collectively referred to as ox tongue. The leaves, often covered with various patterns, grow from a central point and either spiral out like a rosette, or sit opposite one another, almost like a fanned open book. Their pretty flowers are also of note – described less attractively as 'stomach-shaped', they dangle elegantly off long stems.

We love the towering (and eventually trailing) skeletal look of the *Gasteria rawlinsonii*, as well as the often pink-centred, huge and especially tongue-like leaves of the *Gasteria disticha* var. *robusta*. There are many hybrids (some of which are naturally occurring) within the genus and a lot of variability between young and mature plants and species that grow in different environments. *Gasteria* are closely related to *Aloe* and *Haworthia* and are sometimes hybridised with plants from these genera.

CARE LEVEL
novice

LIGHT
bright, indirect

WATER
low

SOIL
coarse + sandy

HUMIDITY
none

PROPAGATION
offsets

GROWTH HABIT
rosette

POSITION
windowsill

TOXICITY
pet friendly

× *Gasteraloe* 'green ice'

COMMON NAME **GREEN ICE**

× *Gasteraloe* is an intergeneric hybrid genus of, you guessed it, *Gasteria* and *Aloe*. This hybridisation between two genera to create a new genus is rare (such an occurrence is signified by an '×' preceding the species name). Green ice is a true mix, looking more like a *Gasteria* when young, and maturing into a more *Aloe*-like shape with a rosette habit once established. It has frosted tips and spots that look silver against the plant's green centre. Its tubular flowers grow up a tall stem, adding a pretty colourful burst to the plant.

Although slow growing, the green ice will eventually stretch out to 30 cm (12 in) in the right conditions. They are drought-resistant plants that don't like to have wet feet. If the potting mix stays too moist or if water gets trapped in between the leaves it can lead to fungal infections. To avoid this, aim water directly onto the soil rather than onto the leaves, and keep your plant in a well-ventilated, dry area. Keeping things super simple, you only need to fertilise once during the growing season, and don't stress about pests, as they're pretty resistant to invading hordes. The green ice can also usually tolerate a little less sun than other succulents, making it perfect for a life indoors.

Haworthiopsis

Previously classified as a species within the *Haworthia* genus, *Haworthiopsis* was identified as its own genus after phylogenetic research in 2013. From the same family as *Aloe* (which these plants resemble) and *Gasteria*, *Haworthiopsis* are endemic to Southern Africa, with most species occurring in South Africa. Generally petite in nature, their sweet little rosettes, often with white markings, are towered over by slender stems of small flowers.

We love the rope-like *Haworthiopsis glauca*, the fun and stripy *H. attenuata* (see opposite), the unusual triangular leaf habit of *H. viscosa* and the starfish-looking *H. limifolia*. The sheer range of leaf shapes, colours and markings will make you want to start a collection to fully enjoy the diversity of this genus.

CARE LEVEL
novice

LIGHT
bright, indirect +
full sun

WATER
low

SOIL
coarse + sandy

HUMIDITY
none

PROPAGATION
offsets

GROWTH HABIT
clumping

POSITION
windowsill

TOXICITY
pet friendly

Haworthiopsis attenuata

COMMON NAME **ZEBRA CACTUS**

Haworthiopsis attenuata's common name is a little misleading as the zebra cactus is in fact a succulent. Nonetheless, this small plant certainly packs a punch with its thick, tapered, dark green leaves with attractively striped horizontal white markings. While this guy won't exceed heights of 20 cm (8 in) and widths of 13 cm (5 in), most specimens are much smaller in size and are likely to stay that way for a considerable time, due to the plant's slow growth habit.

In its natural habitat, *H. attenuata* usually grows in slightly shaded spots, but indoors, a position with lots of bright, indirect and some direct morning sun is best. Because of its small size and penchant for light, a windowsill position is a good option. In summer, when the weather is warmer and the plant uses more energy, water when half the potting mix has dried out. In winter, wait until the vast majority of soil has dried out before watering again.

You only need to fertilise your zebra cactus once during the growing season, using a succulent-appropriate mix. It regularly produces little pups, creating a clumping growth habit, which you can gently remove and replant in order to propagate your succulent.

Opuntia

The genus *Opuntia* is named after the Ancient Greek city of Opus, where Aristotle's successor, Theophrastus, claimed to have found plants that could be propagated by inserting their leaves directly into the ground. Consisting of 150–180 species of flat-jointed succulents from the Cactaceae family, the genus is actually native to the Americas, growing as far north as Western Canada all the way down to the tip of South America. After careful preparation, the pads, flowers and fruit (from which the genus gets its common name, prickly pear) of all species can be consumed, but some are certainly more tasty than others.

Several species of *Opuntia* have become invasive outside of their native habitats, especially in South Africa and Australia. Prolific growers, *Opuntia* can spread quickly if left unchecked. In areas where it's considered a noxious weed it is illegal to plant it outdoors, and in some cases it is also illegal to sell them due to the invasive impacts they can have on ecosystems. That's not to say that you can't enjoy these graphic, paddled beauties, but it is well worth researching the guidelines on these plants in your area before purchasing.

Opuntia microdasys

COMMON NAME **BUNNY EARS CACTUS**

With perfect spotted pads, the young *Opuntia microdasys* is delightfully reminiscent of a bunny's head complete with ears. With access to lots of direct sun, this miniature cactus, endemic to central and Northern Mexico, makes a happy addition to an indoor jungle.

CARE LEVEL
novice

LIGHT
full sun

WATER
low

SOIL
coarse + sandy

HUMIDITY
none

PROPAGATION
stem cuttings

GROWTH HABIT
upright

POSITION
windowsill

TOXICITY
pet friendly

Be warned: the bunny ears' sweet appearance belies its propensity to cause some pretty serious damage – these guys are armed and dangerous! Rather than spines, bunny ears cacti have dense clusters of glochids, or short prickles, that are thinner than the finest human hairs, and are referenced in the plant's specific epithet *microdasys*, meaning small and hairy. These hairs tend to come off in large numbers upon the slightest touch, causing nasty skin irritation, so trust us when we say handle with care!

In addition to its high light requirement, *Opuntia microdasys* also demands excellent drainage. During active growth in the warmer seasons, water only once its cacti-specific potting mix has completely dried out. In winter this will become far less frequent. Although generally fairly resistant to pests, it may experience attacks from mealybugs and scale. These nasties can be dealt with by removing the offending bugs with a cotton tip soaked in alcohol. As with other *Opuntia* species, bunny ears propagates easily and potted cuttings of this sometimes hard-to-find-cutie make a gorgeous gift for friends.

Opuntia monacantha

DROOPING PRICKLY PEAR

While the drooping prickly pear won't be to everyone's taste, this South American native is wonderfully weird and with lots of bright, direct sunlight and infrequent watering, it can thrive indoors, even producing showy yellow flowers that can grow up to 10 cm (4 in) in mature specimens.

CARE LEVEL
novice

LIGHT
full sun

WATER
low

SOIL
coarse + sandy

HUMIDITY
none

PROPAGATION
stem cuttings

GROWTH HABIT
upright

POSITION
floor

TOXICITY
pet friendly

Particularly in its juvenile state, *Opuntia monacantha*'s knobbly paddles are thinner and, therefore, less structurally firm than other *Opuntia* species, as suggested by its common name. Its drooping stems can appear stretched and misshapen, but this is part of the charm of this kooky cactus. For something even more unusual, there is a dwarf, mutated variant: *Opuntia monacantha* 'variegata', commonly known as Joseph's coat. This rarity is one of the very few naturally occurring white-variegated cacti in existence, but it is fairly common in cultivation.

Low maintenance is the name of the game with this prickly pear. While pruning is not essential, it can certainly be cut back as needed to maintain a desired shape and size. Individual pads can be removed, given time to callus and then easily propagated. Just be sure to protect yourself from their deceptively vicious spines. Always use tongs (preferably covered in sponges or material) to hold the pad as you cut the paddle at the joint with a sharp knife.

Xerosicyos

Endemic to Madagascar and consisting of only three species, *Xerosicyos* are flowering plants in the Cucurbitaceae family alongside cucumbers and zucchini (courgettes). The genus name actually translates from Greek to mean 'dry cucumber', as unlike their vegetable relatives *Xerosicyos* have adapted to a drier climate. Some plants have developed succulent leaves, while others have a prominent caudex that stores water at the base of the plant from which deciduous vines emerge.

Xerosicyos danguyi, or silver dollar vine as it is also known for its flat, round, fleshy leaves suspended from thin stems, is the most commonly cultivated species. This elegant succulent makes a beautiful climbing, twining houseplant if you're looking for something a little more exotic to add to your collection.

CARE LEVEL
novice

LIGHT
full sun

WATER
low

SOIL
coarse + sandy

HUMIDITY
low

PROPAGATION
stem cuttings

GROWTH HABIT
climbing

POSITION
bookshelf or stand

TOXICITY
unknown

Xerosicyos danguyi

COMMON NAME SILVER DOLLAR VINE

If money grew on trees, they might look something like *Xerosicyos danguyi*. An elegant and unusual climbing succulent with round silver-green leaves that grow along a cylindrical stem, the silver dollar vine has a climbing, twining habit that produces delicate tendrils, similar to peas, to facilitate upward growth. Without any support, its heavy stems arch gracefully over the edge of some shelves or from a hanging planter. With plenty of bright light, including at least a few hours a day of direct sun, this sought-after succulent makes a unique indoor plant.

Hailing from the arid regions of Madagascar, this drought-tolerant and robust succulent can survive high temperatures, along with extended periods of drought. In a home environment, a potting mix specific to cacti and succulents is best. Allow the soil to dry out between watering in spring and summer, and reduce this even further in winter. All in all, the silver dollar vine is a fantastic option for those just starting out on their indoor gardening journey (if you can get your hands on one!).

specimen *Kalanchoe orgyalis*

Kalanchoe

First described in the 18th century by French botanist Michel Adanson, the *Kalanchoe* genus consists of around 125 highly diverse tropical succulents. Some *Kalanchoe* look more closely related to leafy foliage plants than succulents, such as the *Kalanchoe blossfeldiana* with its shiny green leaves and mass of warm-coloured flowers. While most species grow a manageable one metre (3 ft, 3 in) tall, the *Kalanchoe beharensis* can reach heights of 6 metres (20 ft). There's also the creeping/trailing *Kalanchoe uniflora*, the spotty, stiff grey leaves of the *Kalanchoe rhombopilosa* and the pretty red clusters of downward-facing flowers and coin-like leaves of *Kalanchoe marnieriana*.

Although plants within this genus have some uses in traditional medicine, *Kalanchoe* are mildly toxic and should be kept away from pets and children.

Kalanchoe gastonis-bonnieri

DONKEY EARS

The large leaves of *Kalanchoe gastonis-bonnieri* are grey-green, sometimes tinged with red and spotted with subtle brown markings. They also often look like they've been dusted with white powder. Native to Madagascar, this is a fast-growing succulent, which can reach heights and widths of up to 45 cm (18 in).

CARE LEVEL
novice

LIGHT
bright, indirect +
full sun

WATER
low–moderate

SOIL
coarse + sandy

HUMIDITY
none

PROPAGATION
offsets

GROWTH HABIT
rosette

POSITION
windowsill

TOXICITY
toxic

Typically, donkey ears is monocarpic, meaning it dies once it flowers, but fear not! When the plant reaches maturity at 4–5 years it will develop sweet little plantlets along the tips or edges of its leaves that will live on after the main plant dies. These plantlets send out roots, making them easy to propagate by gently detaching them from the mother plant and potting up in a fresh planter. On average, donkey ears will live for 10–15 years or so before flowering, so all in all, it's not a bad innings.

Allow half of the plant's potting mix to dry out between drinks in summer, and allow all of it to dry out in winter. Never let your plant sit in a saucer filled with water, and keep an eye out for mushy leaves or stems, as this is a sign of over-watering, which could be fatal. Make sure your donkey ears gets some direct sun, with lots of bright, indirect light for the remaining daylight hours. Fertilise fortnightly in spring and summer with a half-strength succulent-friendly fertiliser – this is especially important when the plant is blooming and requires the extra energy.

Kalanchoe luciae

COMMON NAME **FLAPJACK**

Native to South Africa, Lesotho, Botswana and the Kingdom of Eswatini (formerly Swaziland), this attractive succulent has paddle-shaped leaves that can grow to just over 20 cm (8 in) long.

CARE LEVEL
novice

LIGHT
bright, indirect +
full sun

WATER
low

SOIL
coarse + sandy

HUMIDITY
none

PROPAGATION
offsets

GROWTH HABIT
rosette

POSITION
covered balcony

TOXICITY
toxic

Resembling clam shells, these grey-green leaves with their powdery 'bloom' (which protects the plant from overly bright conditions) are complemented by a strong red blush that appears only if the plant is receiving enough light. Flowers appear at the end of winter or early spring on a stalk that can be up to one metre (3 ft, 3 in) long. Sometimes the central rosette can die after flowering, but given that they are unlikely to flower when growing inside, this isn't such a concern for indoor gardeners.

During summer, *Kalanchoe luciae* will enjoy a moderate amount of water and a dose of half-strength fertiliser every month or so until the weather cools. At this point, you should stop feeding your plant entirely and only water once all of the potting mix has dried out. It doesn't like extreme cold temperatures (anything below 0°C/32°F or regular harsh frosts), so it's best to bring your plant inside for winter if it usually lives outside; just be sure to pop it in a bright spot.

Although relatively pest resistant, *K. luciae* can be targeted by aphids and mealybugs, so always keep an eye out and act quickly before they have a chance to take hold. Note that this plant is often mistaken for *Kalanchoe thyrsiflora*, which has similar care requirements but much less of the colourful red edging.

Stapelia

Easy on the eye, less so on the nose, *Stapelia* is a genus of around 50 clump-forming, spineless stem succulents featuring some of the most interesting and infamous blooms going. It is the intricately patterned and textured flowers, with their noteworthy odour of rotting flesh (the sweetly scented *Stapelia flavopurpurea* is the exception), that are the five-pointed stars of the show. Hailing from regions of Africa where there are no native pollinating bees, the glorious, yet smelly blooms serve to attract ants and flies to perform this vital role instead.

A handful of *Stapelia* species are commonly grown as pot plants. Planted in a well-draining potting mix, watered sparingly and positioned with access to plenty of direct rays, these sun lovers can thrive indoors or on a sunny balcony. They are the perfect conversation starter for indoor gardeners of all levels.

CARE LEVEL
novice

LIGHT
full sun

WATER
moderate

SOIL
coarse + sandy +
well-draining

HUMIDITY
none

PROPAGATION
stem cuttings

GROWTH HABIT
clumping

POSITION
windowsill

TOXICITY
toxic

Stapelia grandiflora

COMMON NAME **CARRION PLANT**

With a common name like carrion plant you get a pretty good idea of what you might be in for with this pungent beauty. The *Stapelia grandiflora* is an erect succulent with soft, velvety stems that are generally pale green, but can develop a reddish tinge with lots of direct sun. It is the noxious star-shaped blooms that form at the base of this clumping plant for which this species is both admired and admonished in equal measure, and which gives the *S. grandiflora* its common epithet. Despite all the fuss, the scent is thankfully not overpowering to humans and you need to get up close and personal to get a really good whiff.

Native to the dry, harsh landscape of Southern Africa, the carrion plant's stems provide a crucial storehouse for nutrients and moisture that ensure survival with limited access to water. These stems allow *Stapelia grandiflora* to expand and contract, appearing flat or sunken during times of drought and plump and full when watered. Its flowers also serve a useful purpose in attracting pollinating flies and ants in a region devoid of bees.

The main care requirements of the carrion plant are plenty of direct rays and a coarse, well-draining potting mix. Water deeply in spring and summer, allowing the potting mix to completely dry out in between. You will barely need to water at all in winter, which certainly makes them a low-maintenance plant buddy.

Rhipsalis

Rhipsalis is a genus of about 40 species of abundantly branching succulents commonly known as mistletoe or coral cactus. They are predominantly epiphytic, growing high up in trees (although some are also known to grow in the crevices of rocks), in the tropical and sub-tropical regions of Central and South America. Curiously, one species, *Rhipsalis baccifera* (see page 380), has been found in Madagascar, puzzling scientists who have long theorised over the anomaly.

Having adapted to the humidmoist conditions of the rainforest, jungle cacti differ considerably in appearance and care requirements from their desert-dwelling relatives. The pendulous succulent stems of *Rhipsalis* species take on a plethora of forms, from cylindrical to angular or flattened, and in a variety of thicknesses. From mounding varieties, such as *R. heteroclada*, which resemble clumps of coral, to the flat serrated stems of *R. goebeliana* (see page 383), there's one to suit every taste. A few species have short bristly spines, although most have none at all.

Rhipsalis baccifera

COMMON NAME MISTLETOE CACTUS

Like humans, some plants just have chutzpah and *Rhipsalis baccifera*, with its dramatic mass of thin stems that cascade beautifully, is one such plant. Display this trailing stunner in a hanging basket or on a shelf with plenty of room for its stems to stretch out.

CARE LEVEL
novice

LIGHT
bright, indirect

WATER
moderate

SOIL
well-draining

HUMIDITY
medium

PROPAGATION
stem cuttings

GROWTH HABIT
trailing

POSITION
bookshelf or stand

TOXICITY
pet friendly

In addition to its luscious locks, it produces dainty white flowers that are followed by berries, similar to that of traditional mistletoe from which the plant gets its common name. There really is a lot to love about this easy-care indoor beauty.

A species of jungle cacti, *Rhapsalis baccifera* has acclimatised to a moist, humid environment with light filtered through dense tropical jungle cover. As such, it will not do well in desert-like conditions, and while it will enjoy some direct morning or late afternoon sun, anything more will burn its stems, so keep the light bright, but mostly indirect. Its water needs are certainly higher than those of desert cacti, but it does like its potting mix to dry out at least 5 cm (2 in) between drinks. In its natural habitat, the mistletoe cactus will typically grow in pockets of moss or debris in the nook of a tree branch or rock, so it has adapted to grow in a media that is prone to drying out. To stave off root rot, cut back on watering substantially during winter and always ensure adequate drainage.

The brittle stems of the mistletoe cactus can be easily knocked off when repotting, but fear not as they can be easily propagated. Allow the ends of the stems to callus over for a few days, then pop in a tray with some cacti potting mix. After a few weeks positioned in partial shade, they should be ready to pot up.

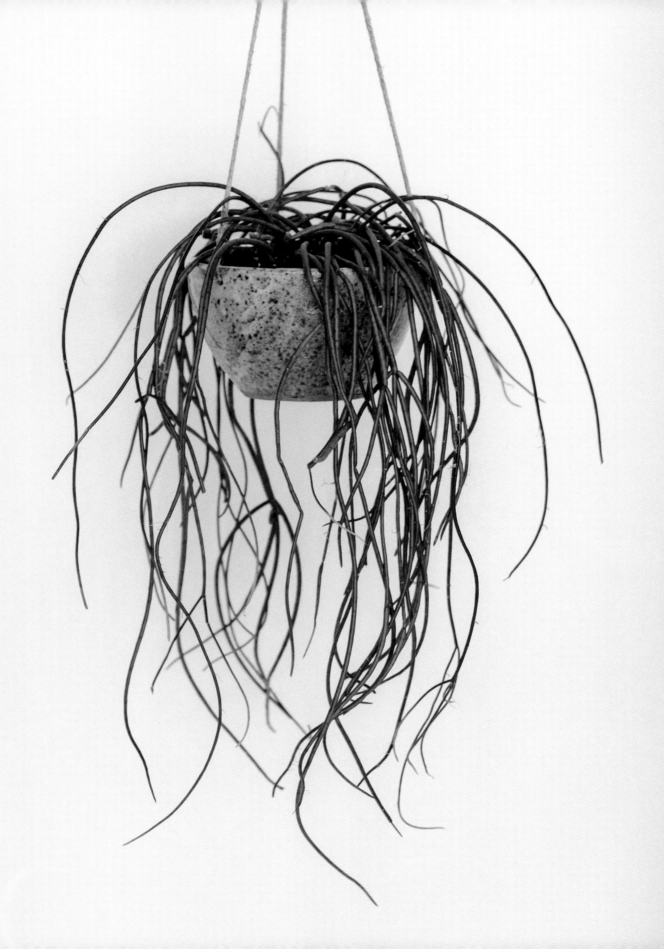

Rhipsalis goebeliana

COMMON NAME FLAT MISTLETOE CACTUS

Haphazard and aimless seems a rather negative description for this kooky epiphyte, but we certainly don't see it that way, and instead rejoice in its chaotic growth habit.

CARE LEVEL
novice

LIGHT
bright, indirect

WATER
moderate

SOIL
well-draining

HUMIDITY
medium

PROPAGATION
stem cuttings

GROWTH HABIT
trailing

POSITION
bookshelf or stand

TOXICITY
pet friendly

Certainly one of the rarer *Rhipsalis*, the smooth flat stems of the *Rhipsalis goebeliana* are slightly serrated around the edges and grow in sections, branching and changing direction at will, and reaching up to an impressive 2 metres (6 ft, 6 in) in length. To top off its sculptural silhouette, the plant produces yellow blooms that turn white upon opening.

German horticulturist Curt Backeberg, known for his collection and classification of cacti, described *R. goebeliana* in 1959 based on a cultivated specimen of unknown provenance. While *R. goebeliana* resembles *Rhipsalis cuneata* and *Rhipsalis oblonga* (both native to Brazil and the Andean region of South America), recent DNA tests indicate that it is not linked to either species and, as such, its habitat remains unknown. Regardless, like all *Rhipsalis* it prefers bright, indirect light and a well-draining potting mix. While this mistletoe species does appreciate humidity, it will generally do well in regular household temperatures and conditions.

Rhipsalis pilocarpa

COMMON NAME **HAIRY STEMMED RHIPSALIS**

Tiny fine white hairs cover the multi-branched pendulous stems of the textural *Rhipsalis pilocarpa*, giving it the common name hairy stemmed rhipsalis.

CARE LEVEL
novice

LIGHT
bright, indirect

WATER
moderate

SOIL
well-draining

HUMIDITY
medium

PROPAGATION
stem cuttings

GROWTH HABIT
trailing

POSITION
bookshelf or stand

TOXICITY
pet friendly

Growing high up on tree branches in tropical rainforests in and around Brazil, sadly this rhipsalis' habitat is threatened by expanding agriculture and urbanisation, and it is now listed as a vulnerable species in the wild. It is, however, popular in cultivation as it grows happily indoors where its clumps of thin stems are prized, with a Royal Horticultural Society's Award of Garden Merit to prove it.

The stems of *Rhipsalis pilocarpa* begin erect, becoming pendant as they grow, branching out in a spiral arrangement. Delightfully fragrant flowers form at the end of its branches and it also produces small, red, bristly berry-shaped fruit. This particularly attractive tropical epiphyte does not love exposure to direct afternoon sun, which can burn its pale green stems, turning them yellow. Having said that, it does enjoy lots of bright, indirect light as well as some direct morning and late afternoon rays. Water your *R. pilocarpa* deeply, allowing the top 5 cm (2 in) of potting mix to dry out in between watering.

Sedum

Commonly known as stonecrops for their seeming ability to grow out of rocks, *Sedum* is a large genus of flowering plants in the Crassulaceae family. While it was once thought that the genus contained as many as 600 species, more recent reclassification has reduced that number to between 400 and 500, with some species shifted to the *Hylotelephium* and *Rhodiola* genera.

Encompassing both creeping and shrub-like growth habits, this group of leafy succulents have the ability to store water in their fleshy foliage. This serves them well in their arid native habitats in Africa and South America. These drought-tolerant beauties are commonly used as ground cover in dry gardens, but a number of species make excellent container and houseplants.

CARE LEVEL
novice

LIGHT
bright, indirect

WATER
low

SOIL
well-draining

HUMIDITY
low

PROPAGATION
stem cuttings

GROWTH HABIT
trailing

POSITION
bookshelf or stand

TOXICITY
pet friendly

Sedum morganianum

COMMON NAME **DONKEY'S TAIL**

Sporting unique trailing stems covered in plump, tightly compacted leaves, the *Sedum morganianum*, or donkey's tail as it is commonly known, makes a beautiful, easy-care succulent both indoors and out. This pendulous plant, with thick stems that appear woven or plaited, adds lovely texture to an indoor jungle. We also love it for its colouring, which can range from a soft lime green to a blue-green, as well as the slight chalky matte finish of the foliage.

Storing water in its fleshy leaves, donkey's tail is fairly drought tolerant and will prefer drier conditions to having soggy feet. Use a potting mix specific to cacti and succulents that will facilitate good drainage, and allow the soil to fully dry out between watering. Particularly important indoors is access to plenty of bright light, including at least a few hours of direct morning sun. Protection from harsh afternoon sun, especially when magnified through a glass window, is advised to avoid leaf burn.

S. morganianum produces delightful hanging clusters of red, yellow or white flowers in late summer. Donkey's tail is perfect for shelves and plant stands, where its trailing growth (up to 90 cm/ 3 ft long) can be displayed and admired.

Selenicereus

Named after the Greek moon goddess Selene and commonly known as moonlight cacti for their beautiful nocturnal blooms, *Selenicereus* is a genus of around 20 primarily epiphytic, but also some lithophytic and terrestrial vine-like, cacti. They grow in the wild from Mexico down through Central America, the Caribbean and into South America. Their mainly flat and jagged stems tend to grow aerial roots to aid climbing, and while some are spineless, other species pack some pretty serious protection.

The large white flowers for which the genus is renowned are some of the biggest in the cactus family and are beautifully fragranced. Pollinated by moths, the special blooms burn bright but extinguish quickly, in most cases lasting only one night.

CARE LEVEL
novice

LIGHT
bright, indirect

WATER
moderate

SOIL
well-draining

HUMIDITY
medium

PROPAGATION
stem cuttings

GROWTH HABIT
trailing

POSITION
bookshelf or stand

TOXICITY
toxic

Selenicereus chrysocardium

COMMON NAME **FERN LEAF CACTUS**

Bold zig-zag 'leaves' that can grow up to 2 metres (6 ft, 6 in) long give this epiphytic, spineless cacti some serious cred. Its graphic stems are selling point enough, but the kicker is in its equally gorgeous flowers, which are delicate and fleeting beauties with stunning golden stamens that are referenced in the plant's Latin name (*chrysocardium* translates as golden heart). Often choosing to bloom by the light of the moon, these flowers are a spectacular sight that, as with so many beautiful things, are sadly short-lived. *Selenicereus chrysocardium* is unlikely to bloom inside anyway, but rest assured its striking foliage is more than enough reason to purchase one.

The fern leaf cactus is actually a jungle cactus that has evolved from a drought-tolerant desert dweller to the humid, shadier climes of the jungle. When this species moved to the tropics, moisture retention was no longer an issue and finding the light became more important, so it spread its leafless stems wide to aid photosynthesis.

Unlike desert cacti, direct sun, except for some gentle morning sun, is a no-no, so keep the light bright but mostly indirect. Water regularly once the top 2–5 cm (¾–2 in) of its well-draining potting mix has dried out in spring and summer, but let the soil almost fully dry out in the cooler months.

Glossary

AREOLE A small bump or depression from where cactus spines grow. A helpful identifying feature of the Cactaceae family.

BRACT Sometimes confused with flowers, bracts are actually modified leaves from where flowers or inflorescence appear on some plants. Their purpose is to attract pollinators or protect the flower. A familiar example of a bract is the white spathe, which gently cups the inflorescence on a *Spathiphyllum* (peace lily).

CACHEPOT Pronounced 'cash-poh', this is a French term that describes a decorative planter without a drainage hole, in which you place a smaller pot that does have a drainage hole.

CAUDEX A swollen trunk, stem or above-ground root system that has evolved to help plants in harsh climates store water. Caudiciform plants are commonly referred to as 'fat plants'.

CHLOROSIS (ADJ. CHLOROTIC) A condition where leaves fade to yellow because they are not producing enough chlorophyll. Some of the more common causes include damaged or compacted roots, poor soil drainage, nutrient deficiencies or a vastly incorrect pH of the potting mix.

CULTIVAR A plant that has been specifically cultivated by humans.

DIGITATE A term used to describe a leaf that is shaped like a human hand.

EPIPHYTE A plant that grows on other plants (usually trees), without the need for soil. They are generally non-parasitic to their host.

FAMILY In the botanical world, family denotes a collection of plants that are grouped according to shared characteristics. There are currently several hundred known plant families, and in the world of taxonomy family sits above genus and species, but below kingdom, class and order.

FORM A particular rank in taxonomy, form sits below species and variety, making it an infraspecific taxon.

FROND A term to describe the divided leaf or leaf-like structure of ferns and sometimes palms, too.

GENUS (PL. GENERA) In taxonomy, genus refers to a group of plants that share the same characteristics. Genus sits below family and above species, and is always identified with italics and a capital letter (e.g. *Monstera*).

HABIT A habit refers to a plant's general structure and appearance. For example: bushy or upright.

HEMI-EPIPHYTE One of two categories of epiphyte (*see also* Holo-epiphyte), hemi-epiphytes only spend part of their life cycle as an epiphyte, either starting life on another plant before making their way to the ground, or beginning life on the ground and making their way up a host.

HOLO-EPIPHYTE The second category of epiphyte, these plants spend their whole lives in or on other plants, never making contact with the ground.

HYBRID The result of cross pollinating two species of plants within the same genus. Hybridisation can also occur naturally in the wild. All plants can be used to make hybrids, including varieties, cultivars and other hybrids.

INFLORESCENCE Unlike a single structure flower, inflorescence is a cluster of flowers arranged on a stem. It may consist of a single or multiple branches.

INFRASPECIFIC A taxonomic rank that sits below species, e.g. variety, subspecies, form or cultivar.

LEAF MARGIN The border or edge of a leaf. A leaf margin might be serrated or lobed.

LINEAR Denotes a long, thin leaf.

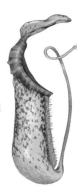

LITHOPHYTE A type of plant that grows on stone or rock without the need for traditional soil. Lithophytes are often found on cliff faces.

LOBE A part of a leaf that is both deeply indented and outdented (can be rounded or pointed).

MIDRIB A large central vein that runs along the middle of the leaf.

MUCILAGE A sticky substance all organisms produce in one way or another. In plants it is often used to help store food and water, and in carnivorous plants it often acts as part of the lure and trap for unsuspecting prey.

MUTATION A naturally occurring phenomenon whereby genes mutate and cause a sudden change in the appearance of a plant. These mutations are often highly valued in the plant world and are cultivated as such.

NODE A generally ridged part of a plant's stem, which in many plants holds all the genetic information from which a new plant can grow. It is the location from where leaves, branches, flowers and/or adventitious roots appear.

OBOVATE An egg-shaped leaf with the thinner end at the base.

OVATE An egg-shaped leaf with the wider end at the base.

PALMATE A leaf with five or more lobes, with midribs radiating from one central point resembling a hand.

PALMATIFID A leaf that has many lobes, with even incisions that only extend less than halfway towards the petiole.

PEDUNCLE The stalk that supports a plant's inflorescence.

PELTATE A leaf with the stalk or petiole attached to its underside, which gives the leaf a shield-like look.

PERFOLIATE A bract or leaf that encircles the node, making it appear as if the stem travels straight through the leaf itself.

PETIOLE The stem of a leaf, attached to a more central stalk.

PINNATE Resembling a feather, a pinnate leaf consists of smaller leaflets arranged on either side of a common petiole. It is common in ferns.

PINNATIFID Pinnate-like leaves, but with lobes that are substantially connected to a petiole, so much so that they aren't considered separate leaflets.

RHIZOME (ADJ. RHIZOMATOUS) A collection of generally underground creeping stems that produce both shoots and roots.

RUNNER Similar to a stolon and a rhizome, this slender stem produces roots and sometimes small shoots, generally above ground.

SCANDENT Growing in a climbing habit.

SERRATE A jagged leaf margin that looks like sharp little teeth.

SPADIX A slender, fleshy inflorescence covered in a cluster of small flowers, most commonly found in the Araceae family (with a spathe) and Piperaceae family (without a spathe).

SPATHE A large protective bract that grows from the base of a spadix. A common example is the single white petal-looking bract seen in *Spathiphyllum* (peace lilies).

STOLON Horizontal creeping stems that grow above ground and send out new roots at various points along their length to grow new plants.

SUBSPECIES A taxonomic category that sits below species but above variety, and identifies plant groups with small differences in features, usually caused by geographical disparity.

SYNONYM Identifies the previous name of a species that is no longer accepted. For example, *Sansevieria trifasciata* is a synonym of *Dracaena trifasciata*, and as such is written as *Sansevieria trifasciata* syn..

TERRESTRIAL A plant that grows from the ground rather than aquatically or epiphytically.

TRICHOMES A diverse range of fine hair- or scale-like growths on plants.

TUBER (ADJ. TUBEROUS) An underground organ that stores water and food. It also protects plants from harsh conditions.

VARIETY A taxonomic category that displays some kind of variation from the true species. It sits below species but above subspecies and form and is noted by 'var.'.

Visual index

NOVICE

Aeschynanthus radicans
LIPSTICK PLANT

Aglaonema 'stripes'
CHINESE EVERGREEN

Aloe × 'Christmas carol'
CHRISTMAS CAROL ALOE

Aloe polyphylla
SPIRAL ALOE

Anthurium scandens
PEARL LACELEAF

Anthurium vittarifolium
STRAP LEAF ANTHURIUM

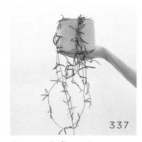

Begonia maculata
POLKA DOT BEGONIA

Bowiea volubilis
CLIMBING ONION

Chlorophytum comosum
SPIDER PLANT

Cereus hildmannianus
'monstrose'
MONSTROSE APPLE CACTUS

Cereus repandus
PERUVIAN APPLE CACTUS

Ceropegia linearis
STRING OF NEEDLES

Ceropegia woodii
CHAIN OF HEARTS

Crassula ovata
JADE PLANT

Cissus rhombifolia
GRAPE IVY

Cotyledon tomentosa
BEAR'S PAW

Crassula perforata
STRING OF BUTTONS

Cremanthodium reniforme
TRACTOR SEAT PLANT

Curio radicans
STRING OF BEANS

Dioscorea sylvatica
ELEPHANT'S FOOT YAM

Dischidia ovata
WATERMELON DISCHIDIA

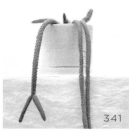

Disocactus flagelliformis
RAT TAIL CACTUS

Dracaena marginata
MADAGASCAR DRAGON TREE

Dracaena trifasciata
SNAKE PLANT

Echeveria × 'Monroe'
MONROE

Epipremnum aureum
DEVIL'S IVY

Euphorbia ingens
CANDELABRA TREE

Euphorbia tirucalli
FIRESTICKS

Euphorbia trigona
AFRICAN MILK THISTLE

Ficus benghalensis 'Audrey'
BENGAL FIG

Ficus binnendijkii
SABRE FIG

Ficus elastica
RUBBER PLANT

Ficus petiolaris
ROCK FIG

Fittonia albivenis
NERVE PLANT

× *Gasteraloe* 'green ice'
GREEN ICE

Haworthiopsis attenuata
ZEBRA CACTUS

Homalomena rubescens 'Maggie'
QUEEN OF HEARTS

Howea forsteriana
KENTIA PALM

45

Hoya carnosa
WAX PLANT

46

Hoya carnosa × serpens
'Mathilde'
HOYA MATHILDE

49

Hoya carnosa var. compacta
INDIAN ROPE HOYA

265

Huperzia squarrosa
ROCK TASSEL FERN

372

Kalanchoe gastonis-bonnieri
DONKEY EARS

375

Kalanchoe luciae
FLAPJACK

285

Lepidozamia peroffskyana
SCALY ZAMIA

281

Livistona chinensis
CHINESE FAN PALM

75

Monstera deliciosa
SWISS CHEESE PLANT

365

Opuntia microdasys
BUNNY EARS CACTUS

79

Monstera siltepecana
SILVER LEAF MONSTERA

268

Nephrolepis biserrata
'macho'
MACHO FERN

366

Opuntia monacantha
DROOPING PRICKLY PEAR

243

Oxalis triangularis
PURPLE SHAMROCK

191

Peperomia caperata
EMERALD RIPPLE
PEPEROMIA

192

Peperomia obtusifolia
BABY RUBBER PLANT

196

Peperomia polybotrya
RAINDROP PEPEROMIA

Peperomia scandens
CUPID PEPEROMIA

91

Philodendron bipennifolium
HORSEHEAD PHILODENDRON

92

Philodendron 'birkin'
PHILODENDRON BIRKIN

95

Philodendron erubescens
'white princess'
WHITE PRINCESS

98

Philodendron hederaceum
HEARTLEAF PHILODENDRON

101

Philodendron hederaceum 'Brasil'
PHILODENDRON 'BRASIL'

102

Philodendron hederaceum var. *hederaceum*
VELVET LEAF PHILODENDRON

106

Philodendron pedatum
OAK LEAF PHILODENDRON

110

Philodendron squamiferum
RED BRISTLE PHILODENDRON

113

Philodendron tatei ssp. *melanochlorum* 'Congo'
CONGO PHILODENDRON

114

Philodendron tortum
SKELETON KEY PHILODENDRON

Pilea cadierei
ALUMINIUM PLANT
61

62

Pilea sp. 'NoID'
SILVER SPRINKLES

65

Pilea peperomioides
CHINESE MONEY PLANT

275

Platycerium bifurcatum
ELKHORN FERN

276

Platycerium superbum
STAGHORN FERN

233

Plectranthus australis
SWEDISH IVY

236

Rhaphidophora decursiva
CREEPING PHILODENDRON

239

Rhaphidophora tetrasperma
MINI MONSTERA

283

Rhapis excelsa
LADY PALM

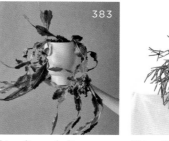

Rhipsalis baccifera
MISTLETOE CACTUS

Rhipsalis goebeliana
FLAT MISTLETOE CACTUS

Rhipsalis pilocarpa
HAIRY STEMMED RHIPSALIS

Schefflera arboricola
DWARF UMBRELLA PLANT

Scindapsus pictus var.
argyraeus
SATIN VINE

Sedum morganianum
DONKEY'S TAIL

Selenicereus chrysocardium
FERN LEAF CACTUS

Spathiphyllum sp.
PEACE LILY

Stapelia grandiflora
CARRION PLANT

Strelitzia nicolai
GIANT WHITE BIRD
OF PARADISE

Strelitzia reginae
BIRD OF PARADISE

Syngonium podophyllum
ARROWHEAD VINE

Tillandsia usneoides
SPANISH MOSS

Tillandsia xerographica
KING OR QUEEN AIR PLANT

Winterocereus aurespinus
GOLDEN RAT TAIL

Xerosicyos danguyi
SILVER DOLLAR VINE

Zamioculcas zamiifolia
ZANZIBAR GEM

GREEN THUMB

Adiantum aethiopicum
COMMON MAIDENHAIR FERN

Adiantum tenerum
BRITTLE MAIDENHAIR FERN

Alocasia clypeolata
GREEN SHIELD ALOCASIA

Alocasia macrorrhizos
GIANT TARO

Alocasia reginula
BLACK VELVET ALOCASIA

Alocasia sanderiana
KRIS PLANT

Anthurium polydactylum
POLYDACTYLUM ANTHURIUM

Anthurium veitchii
KING ANTHURIUM

Anthurium warocqueanum
QUEEN ANTHURIUM

Begonia bowerae
EYELASH BEGONIA

Begonia brevirimosa
EXOTIC BEGONIA

Begonia mazae
MAZAE BEGONIA

Begonia peltata
FUZZY LEAF BEGONIA

Ceropegia ampliata
CONDOM PLANT

Begonia rex
PAINTED LEAF BEGONIA

Caladium bicolor
FANCY LEAF CALADIUM

Caladium lindenii
WHITE VEIN ARROW LEAF

Calathea lietzei
PEACOCK PLANT

Colocasia esculenta
ELEPHANT EAR

Curio rowleyanus
STRING OF PEARLS

Curio talinoides var. mandraliscae
BLUE CHALK STICKS

Davallia fejeenis
RABBIT'S FOOT FERN

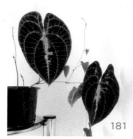

Dioscorea dodecaneura
ORNAMENTAL YAM

Echeveria laui
LAUI

Ficus benjamina
WEEPING FIG

Ficus lyrata
FIDDLE-LEAF FIG

Goeppertia kegeljanii
NETWORK CALATHEA

Goeppertia orbifolia
PEACOCK PLANT

Hemionitis arifolia
HEART-LEAF FERN

Hoya kerrii
SWEETHEART HOYA

Hoya linearis
HOYA LINEARIS

Monstera adansonii
SWISS CHEESE VINE

Monstera deliciosa 'borsigiana variegata'
VARIEGATED SWISS CHEESE PLANT

*Nephrolepis exaltata
var. bostoniensis*
BOSTON FERN

Peperomia argyreia
WATERMELON PEPEROMIA

*Philodendron melanochrysum ×
gloriosum 'glorious'*
PHILODENDRON 'GLORIOUS'

EXPERT

Alocasia zebrina
ZEBRA ALOCASIA

Darlingtonia californica
COBRA LILY

Dionaea muscipula
VENUS FLY TRAP

Drosera sp.
SUNDEW

Nepenthes sp.
PITCHER PLANTS

Sarracenia sp.
TRUMPET PITCHERS

Plant care index

LIGHT

Rhipsalis goebeliana 383
Rhipsalis pilocarpa 384
Schefflera arboricola 241
Scindapsus pictus
   var. argyraeus 203
Selenicereus chrysocardium 389
Spathiphyllum sp. 251
Stapelia grandiflora 377
Strelitzia reginae 141
Syngonium podophyllum 67

MODERATE-HIGH
Adiantum aethiopicum 257
Adiantum tenerum 258
Alocasia clypeolata 207
Alocasia macrorrhizos 208
Alocasia sanderiana 212
Anthurium scandens 171
Anthurium vittarifolium 174
Anthurium warocqueanum 177
Begonia brevirimosa 146
Begonia peltata 153
Colocasia esculenta 217
Cremanthodium reniforme 185
Huperzia squarrosa 265
Monstera adansonii 72
Nephrolepis biserrata 'macho' 268
Nephrolepis exaltata
   var. bostoniensis 271
Oxalis triangularis 243
Strelitzia nicolai 138
Tillandsia usneoides 246

HIGH
Caladium bicolor 158
Caladium lindenii 161
Darlingtonia californica 295
Dionaea muscipula 297
Dioscorea dodecaneura 181
Drosera sp. 287
Hemionitis arifolia 263
Nepenthes sp. 290
Philodendron hederaceum
   var. hederaceum 102
Philodendron melanochrysum ×
   gloriosum 'glorious' 105
Philodendron tortum 114
Sarracenia sp. 299

HUMIDITY

NONE
Aloe polyphylla 323
Cereus hildmannianus
   'monstrose' 305
Cereus repandus 306
Cotyledon tomentosa 349
Crassula ovata 326
Crassula perforata 329
Curio radicans 310
Curio talinoides
   var. mandraliscae 314
Disocactus flagelliformis 341
Echeveria × 'Monroe' 347
Echeveria laui 344
Euphorbia ingens 352
Euphorbia tirucalli 355
Euphorbia trigona 356
Gasteraloe 'green ice' 359
Haworthiopsis attenuata 361
Kalanchoe gastonis-bonnieri 372
Kalanchoe luciae 375
Opuntia microdasys 365
Opuntia monacantha 366
Stapelia grandiflora 377

LOW
Aloe × 'Christmas carol' 320
Begonia mazae 150
Bowiea volubilis 331
Curio rowleyanus 313
Darlingtonia californica 295
Dioscorea sylvatica 182
Dracaena marginata 228
Dracaena trifasciata 231
Epipremnum aureum 55
Hoya carnosa 45
Hoya carnosa × serpens
   'Mathilde' 46
Hoya carnosa var. compacta 49
Hoya linearis 53
Lepidozamia peroffskyana 285
Peperomia argyreia 188
Peperomia caperata 191
Peperomia scandens 199
Philodendron 'birkin' 92
Rhaphidophora decursiva 236
Rhapis excelsa 283

Sedum morganianum 387
Strelitzia nicolai 138
Strelitzia reginae 141
Tillandsia xerographica 249
Winterocereus aurespinus 317
Xerosicyos danguyi 369
Zamioculcas zamiifolia 253

LOW-MEDIUM
Howea forsteriana 279
Livistona chinensis 281

MEDIUM
Aeschynanthus radicans 117
Aglaonema 'stripes' 163
Alocasia reginula 211
Alocasia sanderiana 212
Anthurium scandens 171
Begonia maculata 149
Begonia peltata 153
Ceropegia ampliata 334
Ceropegia linearis 337
Ceropegia woodii 338
Chlorophytum comosum 219
Cissus rhombifolia 223
Colocasia esculenta 217
Cremanthodium reniforme 185
Davallia fejeenis 261
Dioscorea dodecaneura 181
Dischidia ovata 225
Drosera sp. 287
Ficus benghalensis 'Audrey' 120
Ficus binnendijkii 124
Ficus elastica 127
Ficus petiolaris 132
Fittonia albivenis 135
Hemionitis arifolia 263
Monstera deliciosa 75
Oxalis triangularis 243
Peperomia obtusifolia 192
Peperomia polybotrya 196
Philodendron bipennifolium 91
Philodendron erubescens
   'white princess' 95
Philodendron hederaceum 98
Philodendron hederaceum 'Brasil'
   101
Philodendron pedatum 106
Philodendron squamiferum 110

GROWTH HABIT

TOXICITY

General index

A

acanthaceae family: *Fittonia* 134–5
adiantum 254–8
  Adiantum aethiopicum 257
  Adiantum tenerum 258
aeschynanthus 116–7
  Aeschynanthus radicans 117
African milk thistle 356
aglaonema 162–3
  Aglaonema 'stripes' 163
alocasia 205–15
  Alocasia clypeolata 207
  Alocasia macrorrhizos 208
    'stingray' **209**
  Alocasia reginula 211
  Alocasia sanderiana 212
  Alocasia zebrina 215
aloe 319–23
  Aloe × 'Christmas carol' 320
  × *Gasteraloe* 'green ice' 359
  Aloe polyphylla 323
Aluminium plant 61
Angel wings 157
anthurium 165–77
  Anthurium polydactylum 166
  Anthurium scandens 171
  Anthurium veitchii 173
  Anthurium vittarifolium 174
  Anthurium warocqueanum 177
aphids 38
apocynaceae family
  Ceropegia 333–8
  Dischidia 224–5
  Hoya 42–57
  Stapelia 376–7
araceae family
  Aglaonema 162–3
  Alocasia 205–15
  Anthurium 165–77
  Caladium 157–61
  Colocasia 216–7
  Epipremnum 54–5
  Homalomena 200–1

  Monstera 71–9
  Philodendron 88–115
  Rhaphidophora 234–9
  Scindapsus 202–3
  Spathiphyllum 250–1
  Zamioculcas 252–3
araliaceae family: *Schefflera*
  240–1
arecaceae family
  Howea 278–9
  Livistona 280–1
  Rhapis 282–3
  Syngonium 66–9
areole 390
Arrowhead vine 67
asparagaceae family
  Bowiea 330–1
  Chlorophytum 218–21
  Dracaena 227–31
asphodelaceae family
  Aloe 319–23
  Gasteria 358–9
  Haworthiopsis 360–1
Aspidistra 13
asteraceae family
  Cremanthodium 184–5
  Curio 309–14

B

Baby rubber plant 192
Bear's paw 349
begonias 142–55
  Begonia bowerae 145
  × 'tiger paws' **144**
  Begonia brevirimosa 146
  Begonia maculata 149
  'wightii' **149**
  Begonia mazae 150
  Begonia peltata 153
  Begonia rex 154
begoniaceae family: *Begonia*
  142–55
Bengal fig 120

binomial nomenclature
  15–16
  International Code of Binomial
    Nomenclature (ICBN) 16
Bird of paradise 141
Black velvet alocasia 211
Blue chalk sticks 314
Boston fern 13, 271
bowiea 330–1
  Bowiea volubilis 331
bract 390
Brittle maidenhair fern 258
bromeliaceae family:
  Tillandsia 244–9
Bunny ears cactus 365

C

cachepot 390
cactaceae family
  Cereus 302–6
  Disocactus 340–1
  Opuntia 362–6
  Rhipsalis 378–84
  Selenicereus 388–9
  Winterocereus 316–17
caladium 157–61
  Caladium bicolor 158
  'red belly' **159**
  Caladium lindenii 161
calathea 80–7
  Calathea lietzei 83
  Calathea musaica (syn.) 84
  Calathea orbifolia (syn.) 87
  Calathea white fusion 83
Candelabra tree 352
care level 25
Carrion plant 377
Cast-iron plant 13
caudex 390
cereus 302–6
  Cereus hildmannianus
    'monstrose' 305
  Cereus repandus 306

Friendship plant 65
frond 390
fungus gnats 38
Fuzzy leaf begonia 153

G

gasteria 358–9
　× *Gasteraloe* 'green ice' 359
genus 15–16, 390
gesneriaceae family:
　Aeschynanthus 116–7
Giant sword fern 268
Giant taro 208
Giant white bird of
　paradise 138
glossary 390–1
goeppertia 80–7
　Goeppertia kegeljanii 84
　Goeppertia orbifolia 87
Golden rat tail 317
Grape ivy 223
Green ice 359
Green shield alocasia 207
growth habit 31

H

habit 390
Hairy stemmed rhipsalis 384
haworthiopsis 360–1
　Haworthiopsis attenuata 361
Heart of Jesus 157
Heart-leaf fern 263
Heartleaf philodendron 98
heaters 35
hemi-epiphyte 390
hemionitis 262–3
　Hemionitis arifolia 263
history of houseplants 12–13
holo-epiphyte 390
homalomena 200–1
　Homalomena rubescens
　　'Maggie' 201
Horsehead philodendron 91
houseplants
　cultivation 19–21
　growing 25–32

history of 12–13
　trends 13, 19, 20
　see also plants
howea 278–9
　Howea forsteriana 279
hoyas 42–57
　Hoya carnosa 45
　Hoya carnosa × *serpens*
　　'Mathilde' 46
　Hoya carnosa var. *compacta* 49
　Hoya kerrii 50
　Hoya linearis 53
　Hoya Mathilde 46
humidifiers 28
humidity 28
huperzia 264–5
　Huperzia squarrosa 265
hybrid 16, 390

I

Indian rope hoya 49
inflorescence 390
infraspecific 390
International Code of Binomial
　Nomenclature (ICBN) 16

J

Jade plant 326

K

kalanchoe 371–5
　Kalanchoe gastonis-bonnieri 372
　Kalanchoe luciae 375
Kentia palm 279
key 24–32
King anthurium 173
King or queen air plant 249
Kris plant 212

L

Lady palm 285
lamiaceae family: *Plectranthus*
　252–3
Laui 344

leaf cuttings 31
leaf margin 390
lepidozamia 284–5
　Lepidozamia peroffskyana 285
light 25, 35
light meter apps 25
Ligularia reniformis (syn) 185
linear 390
Lipstick plant 117
lithophyte 391
livistona 280–1
　Livistona chinensis 281
lobe 391
lycopodiaceae family:
　Huperzia 264–5

M

Madagascar dragon tree 228
maidenhair fern *see* adiantum
marantaceae family: *Calathea* +
　Goeppertia 80–7
mealybugs 38
midrib 391
Mini monstera 239
Missionary plant 65
Mistletoe cactus 380
Monroe 347
monsteras 15, 71–9
　Monstera adansonii 72
　Monstera deliciosa 75
　Monstera deliciosa 'borsigiana
　　variegata' 76
　Monstera siltepecana 79
Monstrose apple cactus 305
moraceae family: *Ficus* 119–33
mucilage 391
mutation 391

N

nepenthaceae family:
　Nepenthes 289–93
nepenthes 289–91
　Nepenthes sibuy anensis ×
　　talangensis (× red dragon)
　　291
　Nepenthes sp. 290, **292–3**

Contributors

This book would not have been possible without the support and plant-growing passion and prowess of the following people and places.

JANE ROSE LLOYD, HORTICULTURAL CONSULTANT

With a diploma in applied horticultural science and a deep love of plants running through her veins, Jane is a horticulturalist, indoor plant producer, researcher and somewhat all-round botanical genius. Jane owns and operates indoor plant store The Plant Exchange in Melbourne, with her partner, fellow plantsman Michael Chester. Their business specialises in rare and unusual indoor plants, installation and design. We had the pleasure of meeting her when we shot their Melbourne home, which houses a collection of some 500-odd plants, for *Indoor Jungle*. Jane specialises in binomial nomenclature, plant identification and plant selection for niche environments. Her mission to help people foster a positive relationship with plants is one we wholeheartedly connect with.

EDITH REWA, ILLUSTRATOR

Having studied a Batchelor of Arts (Textile Design) at university, Edith is now a highly sought-after illustrator and textile designer. Her stunning illustrations adorn this book, and her love of nature shines through in everything she does.

LATITUDE 23 GLASSHOUSE, ROYAL BOTANIC GARDEN SYDNEY

Sydney's Royal Botanic Garden sits on the harbour's edge, next door to the city's Central Business District. A real oasis, it houses a rose garden, Sydney's fernery, a succulent garden, the National Herbarium of NSW and the famous Latitude 23 Glasshouses. One of these glasshouses is rarely open to the public, and the other not at all, so to have access to both was a real treat. Filled with an incredible array of thriving tropical plants, with rare species of *Anthurium, Alocasia, Philodendron, Nepenthes*, ferns, begonias and many more, we were overwhelmed by the sheer beauty of the collection and the romantic glasshouse setting in which the plants find themselves. LATITUDE 23 GLASSHOUSE'S PLANTS APPEAR ON PAGES 4, 5, 22, 23, 109, 117, 160, 171, 176, 179, 189, 206, 213, 234, 259, 261, 277, 291, 400, 415.

THE CALYX, ROYAL BOTANIC GARDEN SYDNEY

Within the walls of the Royal Botanic Garden Sydney there exists The Calyx, a newly created living art gallery and theatrical experience all in one. At the time of our shoot, the ever-changing living botanical exhibition was home to Plants with Bite, their fourth exhibition, which ran from October 2018 to March 2020 and featured a stunning collection of around 25,000 carnivorous plants. The Calyx hopes to educate and inspire a new generation of would-be plant lovers, horticulturalists and environmental advocates. THE CALYX'S PLANTS APPEAR ON PAGES 287, 292, 293, 295, 297, 299, 411.

ANNO LEON, PRIVATE GROWER

Anno is a DJ, film photographer and grower of an extraordinary collection of plants. We have been avidly following Anno's plant journey for years now. He was generous enough to let us shoot his plant-filled home for our second book, *Indoor Jungle*, and very happily opened his doors to us again to shoot part of his private collection for *Plantopedia*. Anno is an expert propagator and is always willing to share his extensive horticultural knowledge and plant cuttings with fellow plant lovers. His collection of begonias, aroids and hoyas, as well as many other special plants, were styled to perfection by Anno and were an absolute delight to shoot.

ANNO'S PLANTS APPEAR ON PAGES 2, 14, 17, 36, 47, 52, 69, 84, 97, 103, 104, 107, 108, 125, 144, 148, 151, 152, 167, 172, 175, 195, 203, 210, 223, 225, 238, 285, 303, 304, 377, 392.

KEITH WALLACE + GORDON GILES, KEITH WALLACE NURSERY

Best friends Keith and Gordon opened their nursery in 1976. Growing a large range of thriving indoor plants, they are highly regarded for their Cymbidium orchids, ferns and begonias. Gordon is an orchid-breeding specialist who has worked in the industry for over 60 years, while Keith, who was born in Darjeeling, has been growing plants for over 40 years. There is always a warm, welcoming atmosphere at their nursery, with staff treated like family, all sitting down for lunch together every day. Some of their plants were featured in our first book, *Leaf Supply*, and for *Plantopedia* they kindly hosted us at their nursery to shoot both their regular stock and some of the more unusual and rare varieties they are collecting in their private greenhouse.

KEITH AND GORDON'S PLANTS APPEAR ON PAGES 18, 21, 34, 48, 51, 77, 78, 126, 130, 155, 163, 169, 193, 197, 217, 243, 247, 256, 312, 357, 367, 382.

JEREMY CRITCHLEY, THE GREEN GALLERY

Jeremy is the owner-operator of The Green Gallery, a beautiful nursery stocked full of first-rate indoor and outdoor plants. Before launching his business 16 years ago, Jeremy studied horticultural science at university, and gained experience in the industry both in the US and back home in Australia. He regularly travels overseas to visit nurseries and trade shows to keep up to date with plant trends and emerging practices. The team at The Green Gallery are strong believers in the power of the symbiotic relationships found in nature, avoiding harsh chemicals, and instead using beneficial bacteria to keep their plants happy and healthy, which in turn benefits the environment at large. We shot some of Jeremy's plants for *Leaf Supply*, and were generously welcomed at the nursery to shoot for *Plantopedia*.

JEREMY'S PLANTS APPEAR ON PAGES 61, 67, 82, 94, 185, 317, 321, 322, 324, 328, 331, 335, 336, 341, 345, 346, 349, 354, 359, 374, 385.

JACQUI TURK, PHOTOGRAPHER

Jacqui's incredible photographs have appeared in print and online in some of Australia's leading publications, including *Inside Out*, *Real Living*, *Broadsheet* and The Design Files. She perfectly captures the beauty of plants and was an absolute pleasure to work with on *Plantopedia*.

Thank you

We are proud to acknowledge the Gadigal peoples of the Eora Nation as the traditional custodians of the land on which we wrote this book. We pay respects to the Elders both past, present and emerging.

At the launch for our second book, *Indoor Jungle*, our publisher Paul McNally casually suggested a third. We are continually surprised to find ourselves as book authors and we are so grateful for the faith he has in us to continue to deliver beautiful plant books that we so love creating! Thank you, Paul, and the whole team at Smith Street Books for all your support.

To our editor, Lucy Heaver, who has worked patiently with us as we navigated a more in-depth dive into the world of indoor plants, thank you for your guidance and for all your editing prowess.

We send a huge amount of gratitude and admiration to Edith Rewa for her glorious botanical illustrations that really make this book something special.

It was with great relief that we managed to shoot this book just before Covid-19 brought everything to a standstill. It was a pleasure to work with photographer Jacqui Turk who has helped us create the most incredible images that capture the true beauty of plants. We appreciate her enthusiasm, hard work and incredible eye. Along with her trusty assistant, Meg Litherland, they both went above and beyond to get the right shot.

In some ways it has been a blessing in disguise to have a project like this book to keep our minds focused as the chaos of the pandemic swirled around us all. A huge thank you to legends Pia Mazza and Sarah McGrath for holding down the fort at the Leaf Supply studio, while we tried to weather the changing climate alongside putting this book together.

It was a pleasure to be back in the lush homes and businesses of some of our most admired plant people and places. Another opportunity to shoot (and swoon over) Anno Leon's incredible private collection of plants was such a joy. His plant-styling skills are second to none and we're both now converts to the wonders of the plant brush. Shooting at the nurseries of our favourite nurserymen Jeremy Critchley (The Green Gallery) and Keith Wallace and Gordon Giles (Keith Wallace Nursery) felt like a real milestone. We fondly remember venturing out to these businesses and nervously introducing ourselves as we began to source stock for Leaf Supply. Years on and we now count these generous plant lovers as friends who have helped educate us, grow our business and play an important role in the making of our books.

The Royal Botanic Garden Sydney is something of a spiritual place for plant people, and gaining access to shoot not only the Latitude 23 Glasshouses, but The Calyx, too, was such a dream. Thank you to our friend and most peaceful plant person Kate Burton from the Garden for helping to get us in, and to Bernadette and Tanisha for helping to coordinate the shoot and photographic rights.

This book would not have been possible without the specialised horticultural knowledge of Jane Rose Lloyd. Her plant wisdom and encouragement (referring to our plant profiles as 'love notes to plants' made our hearts burst a little) has been invaluable. We hope we can find a way to work with this fabulous plant lady again.

We would also like to thank everyone who has bought one or both of our previous books. It is because of you that we have been able to continue to grow, learn, create and connect with other plant people. All the things we love to do.

On a more personal note, we would like to thank the following people ...

SOPHIA I am so lucky to be surrounded by such supportive and loving family and friends. Thank you to my parents, Janice and Lewis, for looking after Rafi for nearly two weeks straight (on top of everything else they do to help our little family) so I could focus on finishing the manuscript. Thank you to my sister, Olivia, brother, Daniel, and sister-in-law, Trina, for their encouragement and late-night carnivorous plant chat. To Mike and Rafi, I love you. And, finally, to Lauren, for being such a great business, creative and writing partner, there is no way in hell I could do this without you!

LAUREN I would not have been able to take on this exciting but mammoth task without the incredible support of my village. My parents, Maree and Richard, are not only a constant help but my biggest cheer squad, along with my wonderful husband, Anthony, and daughter, Frankie. I love you all. A big thanks to all of my friends and family who have provided endless encouragement and are the first to send me photos of the books in shops all over the world. To Sophia, an excellent business partner, writing buddy and person, Leaf Supply and our books are all the more enjoyable working with you, so thank you.

About the authors

Lauren and Sophia are the co-founders of Sydney-based indoor plant and botanical ware delivery service Leaf Supply, as well as co-authors of *Leaf Supply* (2018) and *Indoor Jungle* (2019). Since publication *Leaf Supply* has been translated into French, German, Finnish, Chinese and Dutch.

Lauren has a background in interior architecture and, along with Leaf Supply, works as an art director. Sophia started life in communications and production before changing track and becoming a floral designer. Together they are totally enamoured by plants and want everyone else to fall in love with them in the same way they have. Their hope is to educate, inspire, build the confidence of fellow indoor gardeners and share their appreciation for the incredible wonder and fragility of our natural world.

Published in 2020 by Smith Street Books
Naarm | Melbourne | Australia
smithstreetbooks.com

ISBN: 978-1-925811-77-3

CIP data is available from the National Library of Australia.

Publisher: Lucy Heaver, Tusk studio
Creative director: Lauren Camilleri
Photography: Jacqui Turk
Illustrations: Edith Rewa
Additional photography: Luisa Brimble, Anna Batchelor, Lauren Camilleri, Lynden Foss, Jessie Ann Harris, Sophia Kaplan, Olivia Kaplan, Janneke Luursema, Aiden Rolls, Lillie Thompson.

Printed & bound in China by C&C Offset Printing Co., Ltd.

Book 146

10 9 8 7

Smith
Street
Books